In Search Of Eden

In Search Of Eden

The Course of an Obsession

by
James Weir

HAUS PUBLISHING
London

Copyright © 2007 James Weir

First published in Great Britain in 2007 by Haus Publishing
Limited, 26 Cadogan Court, Draycott Avenue, London SW3 3BX
www.hauspublishing.co.uk

The moral rights of the author have been asserted.

A CIP catalogue record for this book is available from the British
Library

ISBN 978-1-905791-07-1

Typeset in Garamond 3 by MacGuru Ltd
Printed in Spain by Estudios Gráficos ZURE
Jacket image © akg-Images

For Sarah and John

Pero no quiero mundo ni sueno, voz divina
quiero no libertad, mi amor humano
en el rincon mas oscuro de la brisa que nadie
    quiera
Mi amor humano!

Federico Garcia Lorca
'Poema doble del Lago Eden'

Preface

To adapt a famous saying by my countryman Robert Louis Stevenson – who adapted it in turn from the *haiku* poet Basho – it is often better to travel without apparent purpose than to arrive at some pre-determined destination. It is also sometimes better to travel vicariously than for real, which is why book series like this one exist. Read journeys are often more vivid and always less dusty.

My title is deliberately misleading, and on two counts. What follows is a record of travel, and of a profound human experience that is defined by movement. It is, to some extent, a record of a record, undertaken after trawling through random notes, sketches, diary entries, almost as if I had become the reader of my own experience. Some of what

I read brought back memories at once and with great vividness; others required an effort of recollection; some remained obscure. However, none of the journeys described here were undertaken for the primary purpose of discovering Eden. All were in some way ulterior in nature. I never set out to find the earthly seat of Paradise, and would have regarded such a quest as naïve and beside the point. That is not to say I do not believe Paradise – or Eden – ever existed, merely that I had no conscious intention or hope of finding a place whose existence is unquestionably real and plural (and there is a conclusion to stumble over) but whose deeper reality is mythological and written. Nor should this essay be read as an attempt to return to Eden. The Genesis narrative, which with variations is the fundamental underpinning of all our cultures, has to be taken whole rather than in parts. That means it is a story not just of Paradise, but also of transgression, shame, exile, violence, disaster and chastened recovery.

We all seem to share the dream of a return to Eden. That is the subtext of Stevenson's final sojourn in Samoa, or Gauguin's abandonment of the city for a paradisal Pacific island. It has also been an aspect of my own life in recent years, implicit in a planned but abandoned emigration to the antipodes, but carried out on a tiny farm at home in Scotland rather than New Zealand. Like most dreams, this is one that is compounded not just of wish-fulfilment, but also of memory, anxiety and guilt, a recognition of our fallen state.

The most important journeys are as much interior as physical and mine have combined the two. Only in recollection, and not always in tranquillity, do they seem self-evidently and unmissably connected. Behind this fragmented travel is a restlessness that masks an overwhelming need to put down roots and keeps at arm's length a fatalistic understanding that we are not a species vouchsafed that comfort.

There is, I hope, no self-dramatising tragic strain in what follows. Read through again, its tone is erratically cheerful, at worst bittersweet, and its researches have enough haphazardness to suggest that a lifelong quest has nonetheless been punctuated with enough periods of neglect and indifference to save it from the obsessiveness that – again misleadingly – appears in my subtitle. It is said that the answer to any tabloid headline framed as a question is always no. Here, I hope the answers are 'maybe' and 'yes'. Interrogating the reader is an uncomfortable rhetorical device, but the questions this story poses aren't rhetorical in the usual sense. It is my serious belief – to deliver the premature conclusion again – that Eden was a real aspect of our early existence, but one that has been distilled, symbolically rendered, draped with moral and ethical imperatives that obscure the deeper thrusts of the myth and its connections to felt experience. To accept that Eden exists as text or texts is not to deny that it also once existed as part of a common lot. Narrative has its own internal logic, but almost always some connection to the 'real' world. Anyone who has tired of magazine articles and books with titles and tag-lines like 'Have archaeologists found Paradise?' or 'Did our ancestors plough up the Garden of Eden?' has my sympathy, but not enough sympathy to refrain from posing similar questions. They are the

visible trace of a slow process of recognition, punctuated – as described here – by moments of more
sudden acknowledgement.

Few of these journeys were made alone, but the
contexts and pretexts were too various and too unin-
teresting to make much of the other cast. If fellow-
travellers appear here as anything more substantial
than shadows, as physical enough to be intriguing,
then so much the better. They are by turns sinister,
heart-warming, bothersome and faintly absurd,
linked only by a certain attachment to ideas. If they
seem to belong to that strange freemasonry of adepts
who follow trails of alien abduction, holy bloodlines,
egyptological arcanae and biblical equivalences, they
did not present themselves to me as such. The sole
possible exception – a man you will meet in Chapter
5 – admitted a fascination for such phenomena, but
stoutly argued that his real interest lay in how such
obsessions came to be part of our cultural fabric in the
first place. He warned me that to admit an interest in
the 'real' location of Eden was a kind of professional
suicide. I might just as well, he said, offer descriptions

of the interiors of flying saucers or produce pentacles that aligned obscure Scots and Languedoc churches, strangely shaped hills and enigmatic gravestones. He, though, was the only one with whom I had such conversations. Most of those I met on these journeys were as unaware as I was at the time of their subtext. Those who require to be thanked are acknowledged at the end, as are those writers whose more assiduous researches fed into mine.

There is, I hope, something of Stevenson, something of Rimbaud, not a little of Old Adam and his sons and grandsons in the cracked, curious, faintly posturing fellow you are about to meet.

1

As a young man, I walked for a time in paradise. If Eden ever had an earthly reality, as something more than a mythology of the greatest change in our existence since we stood upright as a species, it surely had more than one location and was part of a rich pattern of common experience, felt by peoples who at the time had little or no knowledge of one another but who later pooled their memories to cement the myth. An unmistakable tug in the blood tells me that one of those storied places lay in the south-eastern half of modern Turkey. I walked there once, and it felt like home. I went back later, and learned that it is our fate to be homeless, no matter how hard we try to put down roots.

There is a consensus, built on some science and

much scrying of the Genesis text, that the Garden of Eden lay somewhere in the once-fertile bowl between the rivers Tigris and Euphrates, in what was ancient Mesopotamia, more recently that curious political exigency we know as Iraq, and in future who knows what? The area offers no shortage of corroborating symbols: the biblical fiery sword reforged as Saddam Hussein's triumphal scimitar or a blackened Russian-built tank engulfed in sand, a jet plane's sheath of missiles or those equally biblical-sounding 'weapons of mass destruction' no one could quite find. If war and internecine hatred, human differences fuelled by fatal knowledge, are the most obvious outcomes of the Fall, then where more obvious as the location of man's banishment from grace than the north shore of the Persian Gulf.

There are other contenders, of course, more or less exotic. For some, the teardrop island of Ceylon – or Serendib – with its Adam's Peak is the likeliest location, and when the tsunami struck in the last days of 2004 that also seemed like an ironic confirmation. Others look to the high plains of Persia,

2

where language and topography seem to conspire in proof. Those who would reconcile biblical and evolutionary versions suggest Eden must have lain in the lush valleys of Eastern Africa where the first modern humans made their tentative way. For a few who look forward to the end of the story, and mankind's return to the paradisal garden, Eden lies in Jackson County, Missouri, where the Mormon pioneers breasted a ridge and saw not just a way-station but a destiny laid out before them.

A better-founded argument, which relies again on synthesis of biblical evidence and some archaeology, sets Eden in the mountains of Eastern Anatolia, in present-day Turkey. It was there I walked in the later summer of 1977, and experienced the strange, soul-moving sense of having in some way returned to the origin of all things. As yet unmet and unknown to me, my first wife and my second – Lilith and Eve, if you will – were also in Turkey when I visited for the first time: the one on what she frankly admitted was a sexual adventure, the other as a young child. For 25 years, I held no expectation of return. Eden is, after all, a place which, once inhabited, one leaves forever and with the chastening bitterness that is life outside the garden, but the memory haunted me daily and ever since, wherever I have settled briefly, in colder and wetter regions, on wind-raked slopes among the hills and on flat sandy plains, on earth that oozes with fertility and on ground that greedily devours any goodness offered to it, I have tried to construct some version of that place. A garden, after all, is where the drama of our encounter with nature is first and most poignantly acted out, where wildness and civilisation meet. A culture or a civilisation can always most easily be defined by its attitude to gardens, or its indifference to them.

⌐

We stopped about noon, breath-catchingly hot. We'd been pulling over on average every hour since sun-up in Gaziantep. The few roads in this south-eastern extension of the Taurus Mountains are – or were – steep, rough and dusty. Everyone looked as if they had been sprinkled with turmeric and smelled as if they had been breaking rocks on a prison line. One of us was travel-sick: monotonous dry retches and muttered apologies. Sometimes the ancient Dormobile needed topped up with water and fuel from the jerricans strapped to the roof. Sometimes it was our driver, a burly Turk with a brigand's face and a laugh like Sid James's, who needed the top-up. His fuel came from the bottles of milky fluid that clanked under his seat and it made his breath smell of aniseed balls. It was a strict regimen, each gulp measured by a filthy thumbnail on the remains of a label, the drinks rigorously alternated with sweet cigarettes, limply rolled in yellowish paper, which seemed to lift his mood and slow his driving to merely reckless.

He was a stickler for lunch, as well, and we were given to understand that this was a longer stop. Mahmout's English was limited to random shouts of 'Coca Cola!', 'Elvis Presley!', 'Malcolm Allison!' (the last always followed by a fake-spit) but he had a repertoire of international gestures – eating, drinking, peeing, fornicating – that made his message

5

unambiguous. Every time we stopped, he turned to what looked like the same greasy copy of *Cümhüriyet* and on straighter stretches of road would flatten a couple of columns over the steering wheel and peer down at football stories – Mahmout's stained shirt was the strident yellow of his team Fenerbahce, hence the dislike for Allison, latest in a run of English managers at rivals Galatasaray – and then up at the bouncing horizon. When it was my ill-luck to draw the passenger seat beside him, unspokenly considered the suicide seat and thus avoided, he would punch my arm or thigh and point to a picture or story. Mostly they were of glamorous sportsmen with large numbers in the caption or headline, presumably transfer stories. Once, though, Mahmout clicked his tongue sharply at something he'd seen and silently handed across the softening pages. On the folded section was a photograph of a young man in uniform kneeling on the ground while behind him what looked like an NCO looped a garrotte round his neck. The wire was already tight on the young man's flesh but there was no sign of pain on his face or emotion on his executioner's. The scene might almost have been posed. Mahmout made the finger-mime for running, inverted digits tapping away across the dashboard, and then bugged his eyes and stuck out his tongue: *ccchhhh!* It was done with absolute matter-of-factness, and as with most of his wordless communications, it made immediate sense. Here was an army deserter, getting his deserts.

We drove some way from the main road, along an even dustier track that seemed to run parallel to our original route. Women and children held neck-clothes over their faces and stared impassively at us. A man of seemingly impossible height and thinness unfolded from a doorway. His height was illusory. It was the door that was tiny, but the visual paradox was heightened by the dark western suit and white shirt the man was wearing. As we passed, he eased back the jacket to show a large pistol stuck into the waistband. Though the gesture came straight from movie westerns it was done, like Mahmout's tiny narrative, without drama and without apparent threat. It simply said, 'See, I have a gun'. It was something we would see often later, further east; as the houses became more primitive, smaller, muddier, the men seemed ever taller, the suits and shirts yet more improbably crisp, the guns ever-present, the whiff of potential violence still subtle but more overt.

Then suddenly the air seemed to soften and cool. Tree shadow wrapped us and Mahmout jolted the van to a halt in front of a building whose single storey seemed to have been roughly eviscerated to leave a dark space filled with tables, a table football machine, and a cabinet fridge of Santa Claus red. 'Coca Cola!' The big, grimy hands again mimed eating, drinking, peeing, spinning football-machine handles; lascivi- ous pelvic jerks and a cocked thumb suggested other comforts might be available through the bead curtain at the back. They stopped at once when the beads leapt and a sour-eyed woman broke through, holding a scarf in front of her mouth, speaking through it, muffled, interrogative, unpleased.

There were movements and whispers behind the curtain as we ate and drank: greasy lamb, chickpeas, flatbreads, Coke and Tuborg lager. Every time there was a whisper or giggle at the curtain, Mahmout jerked his head round, but the girls wouldn't show themselves. He tired of the game and switched his attention to the hubble-bubble pipe an old man brought out to the table. Mahmout fussed with the charcoal and smoked contentedly, breathing out soft clouds of apple-wood smoke which seemed to hang like ectoplasm around his chest. The others descended on the table football machine.

I've never seen the point of football anywhere but on grass, and didn't smoke in those days, so I went outside to walk off the travel-stiffness and the food. No one was around. The only thing that moved was a yellow bitch with swollen dugs who seemed to have trotted across every exotic movie set I had ever seen. She eyed me briefly and trotted on. There were half a dozen other buildings visible, some little more than low huts, one other with the same gutted look as our café, though this one seemed to act as a local garage. An ancient saloon was propped up on stones, tools scattered around where they had been dropped. I had intended to keep our van in view as I walked, thinking of that gun, but something drew me off the road.

I felt it the way a blind person might feel light or sense an open doorway. Illumination that spread across the skin; a liminal promise. I struck down a narrow path, brushing camphorish shrubs, breathing deeper, feeling – there is no other word for it – *suspended*. It was like the moment in jazz when the harmonic tensions have gone past the point where they are heard as conflict, to the point where they are just held in place by the metre and by some expectation of release, suspended and sustained.

I whisper when I walk and think, and when I play piano, vacant mantras that give pulse to the movement. As I moved down the pathway, barely wide enough for my shoulders, increasingly scented by my progress, I began to mutter *Fenerbahce, Fenerbahce, fener bahce, fener bahce.* The district where Mahmout's favourite team was founded must have been the site of one, because *fener* is the Turkish word for 'lighthouse' ...

∽

I'd set off a fortnight before, on an East Coast ferry to Hamburg, watching fingers of light push out from the receding land and then reach out from the Danish and German coast ahead. I made the crossing in the company of a quiet Iranian who chewed his fingernails and seemed nervous at passport control. We met the next of our travelling companions in Hamburg, a slim American whose long hair was just too regulation-long to strike the required note and whose jeans and sneakers looked unconvincingly new. He seemed to run across us by chance at the dockside but his 'You must be ...' suggested a planned rendezvous, even if only he was in on it.

We took the train to Munich, via stops in Hannover and Giessen, towns where Britons and Americans respectively seem to feel at home; then by car down through Trieste where our American companion-driver also seemed to know where to find people; then on to the Istanbul ferry, a slow, dull, mostly silent drive down through the creaking twilight of Tito's Yugoslavia.

There was a lighthouse at Trieste, too, but its

11

light was pale and its period somehow uncertain, as if dwindling. I thought of James Joyce, writing his 'Work in Progress' there, his own light getting dimmer, memories of home fading with his bruised eyesight. There are lights round the Bosporus as well and they seem to spotlight the traveller, as if the next step is always somehow courageous or foolhardy, like Byron's notorious swim. It's said that the German chancellor Konrad Adenauer once muttered '*Ach, Asia*' in his sleep as his night train rattled across the Elbe bridge, but no one who has ever made the journey across the Bosporus from Asia Minor can ever have failed to think that here the East begins. There is a smell, not so much spicy as resiny and like the old East Berlin. The cars seem to smoulder their fuel rather than burn it, leaving an odd tang of hydrocarbons and sulphur in the air.

We met our other companions in Stamboul: another American with the same look of contrived casualness, a slightly older Englishman with a vague, Oxford manner. The Iranian we'll call Sattar. An odd cast, even before we hooked up with Mahmout and his van. Given my lack of funds I'd been disposed to overlook the trip's oddity and ambiguities, or even to address the possible reasons behind it. What made it irresistible was the itinerary, the promise of a bit of pocket money, and the suggestion, which was never entirely explicit, that the whole thing had been arranged by or with my old university friend Kourosh (let that be his name here), a Persian with enamel-black eyes, a ferocious analytic intelligence, no evident money but the kind of easy charm even Scottish women – even Edinburgh women, God help us – found hard to resist.

I met Kourosh at a concert by the improvising group Gentle Fire who were playing at the university. He was there with two red-haired sisters from the New Town, the younger of whom I knew. He was cheerfully mystified by the music and intrigued by my enthusiasm for it. We hit it off. Over the months ahead, we drank, practised English (his, mainly but not exclusively), chased after women, and talked politics and history for hours. He was a political science postgraduate; I was a dabbler. During that

13

time, fuelled by the same unshakable curiosity that had led him to just about double the Gentle Fire audience with his double-date, we visited every literary and cultural shrine, every significant historical site within reach of Edinburgh: Abbotsford and Bannockburn, Adam Smith's birthplace and David Hume's grave, Langholm (he admired MacDiarmid, surprisingly) and, in a borrowed car, Drummossie Moor hard by Culloden House. The city's storied architecture and its hills never held me, though. Even if Arthur's Seat had some convincing connection to the Round Table and the Grail legend; even if the Castle rock were, according to one eccentric 1930s theorist, the real site of Calvary, they seemed to lack mythological bulk. My thoughts were always elsewhere and always focused at earlier points in the human epic. On cold Midlothian nights and in much the way clarinettist Sandy Brown and trumpeter Al Fairweather had once walked those streets singing jazz parts because they had pawned their instruments, I prowled the vennels and wynds with Kourosh, eking out the beer money, holding back enough for a last whisky, keeping warm by reciting all the destinations for which I had neither tickets nor prospect of them: Giza, Masada, Trebizond, Erzurum, Ararat, Van.

Kourosh disappeared at the end of my junior year, his second as a doctoral student. That seemed to be that. A year or so later, I was approached – outside a lecture by A. L. Rowse, of all places – by a quiet but insistent fellow who insisted we go for a drink. I've never been of interest to gay men, and in those innocent days probably knew next to nothing of how that culture functioned, but I have an ear for accents and in those flatted vowels and soft gutturals I recognised the same accent as Kourosh's. My new friend was called Sattar (or will be here). He let it be known that he knew Kourosh and something of our conversations. For the next year, he resurfaced periodically, sometimes borrowing money, sometimes paying it back over the odds and over my protests, sometimes full of questions that never quite seemed to mount up to a conversation.

Then a message came through mutual friends in London that Kourosh was organising, but not himself going on, a trip through Eastern Anatolia. A van load of archaeology 'students' would go from Istanbul to Ankara, then down through the Taurus to near the Turkish border, then round in a sweep to Lake Van, and home via such storied place-names as Erzurum and Trebizond. Kourosh was even able to 'help out' with some money, which was astonishing, since in Edinburgh he had seemed barely solvent. In return, I was to bring Sattar.

I am an archaeologist in the same spirit I am a birder, happy to stand and watch, not enthralled by the prospect of lying horizontal and twitching away grains of dust from potsherds or arrowheads. It was clear that this was not to be that kind of trip but, long before the word had started to sprout worthy and less worthy prefixes – eco-, sexual – an exercise in archae-otourism, with just a touch of *Boys' Own* thrown in, 'knocking about' the old Ottoman Empire in a latter-day version of the Great Game. There was a subtext. I was given to understand that we went out as five and would come back as four. Sattar was 'required' at home in Iran. His exact role was never specified, and nor was there any explanation as to why he could not simply be flown into Tehran. He seemed not so much nervous as keyed on the journey, physically restless, even hyperactive when there was an opportunity – he was the first to rush to the table football machine – oddly passive and unresponsive the rest of the time. Conversation was difficult in the van, but I was disturbed by his unwillingness to talk. If I pointed something out he merely smiled and nodded.

The hand-over was on a quiet road east of Diyarbakir, in the shade of a tree that looked as if it had been wrenched out of the earth and replanted upside down, roots to the sky. We were still three days steady drive from the Iranian border, and still far from Van, where I had been led to believe something would take place. Three men were waiting by a battered truck. One of them, it's hardly a surprise to say, was Kourush. He crushed my hand and smiled with what looked like regret, said nothing. Sattar embraced him and the two others, who might have been Kourush's brothers, though he'd never mentioned any – and waved wanly back at us. As we pulled away, I saw

Sattar pull off his denim jacket and replace it with a jerkin and felt hat that from behind and at a growing distance seemed to change his shape and nature immediately. Kourosh stuffed the 'Western' jacket into a canvas bag, and then dust faded the scene to grey. I never saw either of them again. The Americans said nothing.

Up to then, they'd talked enough for all of us, though rarely to each other. They didn't so much converse, as broadcast. One seemed intent on flashing his knowledge of the region, and hinting at inside knowledge – of local foods and sports like that strange national obsession, *yagli gures* or oiled wrestling, of the fifteen ageing Jupiter IRBMs at Izmir which had been Kennedy's slender bargaining chip during the Cuban missile crisis, though also the confirmation of American hypocrisy – while the other seemed more intent on projecting a broad-spectrum bonhomie that never got beyond the tight New England smile, let alone to the rarely uncovered eyes. My English companion and I did a little fishing, throwing out crudely baited references to 'the Company', or even

'Did you ever try that pub in King's *Langley?*' Once, after too much Tuborg, things got even more foolish: 'I think that was the *Dulles*-t village we've seen yet' or dropping 'Castro', 'Baia de Cochones' into macaronic, or just moronic, Spanish-French routines – sub-so-phomoric stuff, and to their credit the Americans paid it not the least notice. Whether they were CIA, I neither knew or cared, and care less now. They seemed in possession of secrets, spoke with the inconsequential gravity of the initiated; they were *something*. What troubled me more was that I had found a lost friend and lost him again in an instant; what was terminal in that sudden handclasp on a hot road was the knowledge that this was all part of something ordained elsewhere, that whatever he was, Kourosh was controlled by a purpose larger than friendship. If he was lost to me, it seemed he might also be lost to himself.

None of this was in mind on our final night in Istanbul. We ate cheaply and well in a café near the Blue Mosque, the area full of young Americans, occasional Britons, embarked on the Hippy Trail. By some unspoken collective agreement, we remained pretty much silent as we ate and drank, eavesdropping conversations at other tables, volunteering nothing when a pretty girl with a heavy Black Country accent shouted a question about exchange rates, lira to sterling, or when a group of young men suddenly exploded into grunting scuffles, the cause obscure, the purpose of their slow, clumsy wrestle back and forth across the café floor, bumping tables, spilling drinks, never clear. We sat and watched, not conspiratorially, and not with any air of superiority but with the quiet of ulterior purpose.

It was a strange year, 1977, soundtracked by the Sex Pistols, Skrewdriver and *Saturday Night Fever*. The young Englishmen wrestling their way across the café floor weren't the only absurd dancers that summer. Young Turks who'd been watching the Italian dub of *Il febbro de sabbato sera* threw shapes on every street corner. There was horror in the air that year, but there was also comedy in the violence. The spring had seen the world's worst airline disaster, on the ground at Tenerife airport. Magazines reprinted a photograph of a dazed survivor standing looking at the burning wreckage of two 747s, all but the cuffs and collar of his clothes ripped off his back. The scene was terrible; he looked almost clownish. There were other crashes (a burning rash of them), abductions, kidnaps, political assassinations. In Pakistan, General Muhammed Zia al-Haq overthrew prime minister Zulfiqar Ali Bhutto; a Sunni married to a Kurd, Bhutto seemed like a prophetic martyr when he was hanged two years later. Others didn't have to wait that long to achieve iconic status. In Utah, Gary Gilmore was shot by firing squad and became an instant existential hero. Actor Freddie Prinze shot himself. In Milan, a hooded man fired at police; the picture went round the world and his pistol crouch became the year's other iconic pose, after John Travolta's. The space shuttle took off for the first time, but piggy-backing on a jet plane; if the space programme had been the expression of a New Frontier, it had stalled and gone all military-industrial, as well as slightly pathetic. *Star Wars* was released; more bargain-basement iconography, though the title and term soon came to mean something ironically different. Armed Hanafi Muslims took hostages in Washington, DC, an early whisper of that great national *cauchemar* 'Islamic extremism'. There was even an assault on the World Trade Center, when George Willig, 'The Human Fly', took three and a half hours to climb the South Tower. The mayor fined him $1.10, a cent for every storey.

Life itself seemed at a discount. Bhutto's overthrow left him a dead man walking. The latter months of the year also claimed Steve Biko and Elvis Presley, as well as rock band Lynyrd Skynyrd. Even before the air crash that claimed half their number, the band's signature song 'Free Bird' had become a generational anthem compounded of ironic liberation and loss, its endless finale striking a curiously fatalistic, even desperate note. That all came after summer's end, and in a fall that for me seemed a small, private replication of our great Fall. For the moment, drifting away from the café to walk off the food before sleep, I felt disengaged, alert to threat, excited but homesick, my lungs and blood tainted by the year's toxic spills of bad news. The air chilled noticeably, though the streets were still busy. As I walked, snippets of English, otherwise unwelcome, seemed to offer stepping stones of safety through the darkened city, a perverse sanctuary. I stood for a time at the water watching the channel lights flashing their codes. We'd met our driver briefly and had an early rendezvous in the morning. The cadence was almost complete: *fener bahce, fener bahce* ... lighthouse ... garden ...

The path forked, as paths in search narratives are required to do. I took the lower branch, not because anything drew me downwards into the vegetation, but simply because it seemed less effort. The shrubs now met above my head. The air was close and filled with pungent dust. I came to a wall, or at least a stone barrier. Perhaps ten feet high, it was made of stone and mortared with mud or a crude pinkish cement. From any distance that wall must have looked like some anomalous mineral accident, cut by wind or water, thrown up by storm or seismic movement.

Up close, I could see handprints on the surface. the whorls and arches still showing, signatures of human intention.

Again I went left, conscious that my companions were somewhere above me on that side and, anxious lest I miss the emphysemic ignition of the van. After maybe twenty yards the path ahead became more distinct, marked by the passage of feet, and I came to an opening. There was a high threshold stone which meant that I had to bow my head to climb through. I raised it again and was back at the beginning of the world.

The problem with 'garden' is that to a European it signifies a certain kind of order, a clipped and weeded obedience to design. 'Wild' and 'natural' gardens are counter-intuitive or at best contentious, a fashionable ideal that prompts revisionist debate about how wild wilderness actually is and how thoroughly even the densest Amazonian jungle bears the mark of man. This was not a garden in any sense I hitherto understood. The eye almost rejected it in the way the eye fails to register what it has not been programmed to

24

see. Rather, I experienced it as something that struck the other senses in a chord. Simultaneously, I felt a change in the pressure and humidity of the air, an unexpected springiness underfoot, a rich reduction of smells – spice, wormwood, something like melon, something like the tang that comes off brushed tomato leaves, something as earthy and bitter as mocha – and underneath it all, a faint continuo of running water, light as a spinet, accompanying … what? When the composer John Cage stood in the anechoic chamber he expected to experience absolute silence. What he heard instead was the insistent thud of the blood-stream and the hiss of his own central nervous system. Something similar happened in that sudden garden. In the apparent silence, with just those faint liquid trills beneath it, I heard the garden growing.

It has been the basic music of my life ever since, triad, hexachord, soul's tonic, unresolvable and perfectly resolved, ever present and utterly fugitive. I catch whispers of it here and there, in the summer woods in Scotland, buried in otherwise dull ensembles, reached for in improvisations. Since, as

Marconi believed, no sound ever dies, merely becomes infinitely faint, I think of it as the fading birth-cry of the planet itself, like the cosmic whisper of the Big Bang.

Nothing looked planted. There were no rows, no labels, no forcing pots, canes or frames. The plants that crowded that luminous space seemed to have happened there spontaneously, with no sign of that 'quarrel with nature' which Michael Pollan considers definitive of gardening. It was as if I had stumbled across some rich forage in the wilderness, put there by history rather than nurture. Squashes were filling out so fast they were bent into sharp little crooks, fruits were putting on flesh faster than they could harden a skin, pods pregnant with seeds. And yet the impression was changeless rather than dynamic, as if these apparently random plants were here for all time, without weather or season, fixed at some burgeoning moment under an overhead sun.

The light was the strangest thing of all. In the centre of the garden was a tree, a tortured thing held at the most extreme point of some distant arboreal contortion, its upper branches looking like bunches of abandoned umbrellas blown inside out, the smaller ribs almost metallic, the big leaves like torn fabric. Years later, when I worked for a time as a garden designer myself, I would pore over textbooks on the subject and nod sagely at diagrams of shade pattern. I remember one neatly-drawn image of flower- and vegetable-beds to be with the words 'UNWANTED TREE' etched underneath a billowy shape that refused to promise them the light they demanded.

The light was strange because despite the dark monster that squatted in the centre of the garden and sprawled over the surrounding wall, everything around it and even beneath it seemed to occupy its own sphere of luminosity. While the tree seemed to absorb light, the plants gave off their own, vibrant and tactile. The water that bubbled up in a tiny freshet in the corner seemed *available* to the whole garden.

It is always suspect when a writer reaches for music, as if the unsayable can somehow be rendered in another, purer form. In that garden, though, I found myself without language. Not only was nothing

27

labelled, everything seemed to lack its signifier. 'Squashes' is an approximation and an afterthought. There were tomato-like fruits, but they emerged from a papery sheath. There were what might have been aubergines, not the polished purple clubmen we buy in supermarkets and then throw away, unsure, but the paler scions that offer up 'eggplant' as a nickname. There may have been okra, hot peppers, and some feathery clumps may have been carrots, originally prized for their foliage rather than the roots. Everything touched gave off a heated spritz of musk, quickly blending into the last, never quite identifying its olfactory family: citrus, mint, liquorice, gall. This was a time, you must remember, when wrinkled green peppers were still exotica in British shops, but the real point is different. That headlong richness and randomness of growth simply thwarted description, induced a temporary aphasia.

Not so temporary, perhaps. For thirty years I have tried to recover that moment, throwing together gardens in good soil and bad, in sodden wet and in drought, as if instead of describing the place I might be able to replicate it. But human intervention always reveals itself, whether in a neatly taxonomised specimen garden, a more sprawling potager, or in a carefully conserved wilderness. Most of us revert to neatly hoed rows, F1 hybrids, slug pellets, netting and cloches. We are order-making mammals. Whenever I scatter wildflower seeds in a meadow garden, the result is never 'natural' but as gestural and contrived as a canvas by Jackson Pollock. Nature launches guerrilla attacks at the boundaries of a garden, but mostly waits, knowing that human vigilance is limited. Here, precisely, is the paradox and the 'quarrel' that Pollan speaks of. It is also the quiddity that so passionately engages the creationists, the evolutionists and Intelligent Designers. Does the Creation reveal a master plan, or is it merely 'history', the result of trillions of dice-throws? Is 'nature' pre-human and absolute, but subject to our depradations, or is 'nature' simply another aspect of human history, a projection of our need for some ideal Other that exists before and hopefully beyond us, and that doesn't require the complication of a God, other perhaps than as a First Gardener, though that in turn, of course, dents the idea of nature as absolute. And so it goes, round and round …

My wife, a brilliant and passionate photographer, concedes that there are epiphanies of light and shade, cloud formations, oncoming rain, sudden refracted rays at sunset that decline to be captured by a camera and which are best left alone. A writer rarely reaches that position of stoical acceptance. Much can be done in the darkroom and with Photoshop, but words seem infinitely malleable, with that dangerously beguiling *demi-vierge* manner that leads you to believe you might just be able to possess them for the very first time.

This disjointed narrative – disjointed because the journeys it describes were such, and made by a man often seriously out-of-joint with the times, 'narrative' rather than 'story' because the essence is not so much the physical journey as the means of telling it – describes a search for the meaning of that experience and the real-world basis for our memory/dream of Paradise. Sometimes I feel someone has got there before me. Not Milton who set his Eden in an English park. Not any of those anthropologists or exiled fellow-travellers who left a city for the islands and discovered people living in a state of nature. I love Milton, but those others excite my irritation: bad methodology, sentiment, escapism. However, sometimes in unexpected places a voice speaks with the haunted ring I recognise. Thomas Pynchon might seem a writer for whom the very notion of Eden was meaningless, and yet in *Mason & Dixon* Pynchon wrote one of the great historical epics of the American quarrel with wildness. There and elsewhere Original Sin, damnation, banishment and preterition are his great themes. And then in his 2006 novel *Against The Day*, I found this. The man who speaks is the troubled explorer Fleetwood Vibe: 'There are stories, like maps that agree ... too consistent among too many languages and histories to be only wishful thinking .... It is always a hidden place, the way into it is not obvious, the geography is as much spiritual as physical. If you should happen upon it, your strongest certainty is not that you have discovered it but returned to it. In a single great episode of light, you remember everything.' There is much else in the chapter that resonates with me: references to music, to photography, the threatened 'wilderness', the distant haze and smoke of industrial civilisation, the fateful towers of New York (*Against The Day* is in that now unmistakable genre, the 'post 9/11 novel'), the illusory persistence of the nation state, the possibility that round some trail-bend, down some narrow divide in a poisoned landscape, there will be Zion. That last possibility is where the resonance negates, for everything you will read here is premised on the belief that heaven always lies behind us, a source of memory and of consolation, a way of being that can still be grabbed at by the creative mind, but from one which, once born, we are always aware of banishment.

There is a sure giveaway in the prose of anyone who tries to touch on these themes, rolling periods of paratactic phrases, long lists rather than argument, *and, and, and* ... One hears it in Walt Whitman, of whom Pynchon is the perverse descendant, and in the New York poets rhapsodic singing of American reality. One picks it up again in Federico Garcia Lorca, who wrote sleep-walking ballads, an ode to Whitman, and in 'Poema dobla del lago Eden' asks:

> *Dejame pasar la puerta*
> *donde Eva come hormigas*
> *y Adan fecundas peces deslumbrados.*
> *Dejame pasar hombrecillo de los cuernos*
> *al bosque de lose desperezos*
> *y los alegrisimos saltos.*

'Let me pass through the door where Eve eats ants, and Adam fertilizes dazzled fishes. Horned dwarf, let me pass through to the wood of yawnings and stretchings, and of exhilarating jumps.' In another, shorter poem, Lorca finds the first man 'dreaming in the fever of clay' and dreaming of the approaching child …

> *Pero otro Adan oscuro esta sonando*
> *neutra luna de piedra sin semilla*
> *donde el nino de luz se ira quemando.*

'But another obscure Adam sleeping dreams neuter

seedless stone moon far away where the child of light will be kindling.'

There was horror at that garden threshold as well as an episode of light. It was compounded of many things: the childless gloom that only afflicts the old and the uncertainly young; a sense of life as constraint, its freedoms guarded by the horned toad of depression or poverty or political brutality; but also the unbearable experience of, just for a second, *remembering everything.*

The maps do agree, the stories are too consistent. Somewhere in our distant past there was an Eden and our curse is not so much that we do not live there any more as that we are condemned to remember it.

⌒

I walked for a time in that walled garden, breathing the changed air, charged with a feeling more profound than *déjà vu*, perhaps the same feeling an amnesiac has when after months of uneasy loss of self he sits down and discovers he can play the piano or speak fluent

Portuguese. The plants fascinated me. They were not in themselves exotic, indeed quite the reverse. The fascination lay in their interconnection, a fittingness to place and purpose that managed to seem both mundane and uncanny.

There was a quality to the place that seemed not-to-be-spoken-of (perhaps there is an agglutinative German word that says it better, the way *unheimlich* is better than 'uncanny') but I did once or twice try to verbalise the experience. Living in Surrey five years later, I tried to describe it to a doctor friend. She was also a keen orchid grower, who openly preferred her hypochondriac *Cipripediae* and *Aurolicholiae* to her genuinely ill patients. 'Sounds like an epileptic aura', she said, 'We might want to look into that.'

If that is what it was – and we never did look into it – then the premise of this quest is different. On the other hand, too much modern medical debunking of ancient and medieval visions, the product, they now tell us, of starvation, hypermenorrhea, migraine or ergot poisoning, ignores what comes riding in on such 'hallucinations'. Here again, the stories are too consistent to ignore, even if the mapping of the brain still hasn't got past the '*here bee monsters*' stage. The whole quibble about Eden is whether it was a real place or a state of mind, an actual garden or an elaborate evolutionary metaphor. So committed are we to deconstruction, we forget the plainer possibility that both might be true, an edifice of mythology built on the founds of historical or empirical fact, just as a real Osiris and an all-too-physical Set may once have wrestled in the hot desert and only later been turned into gods. If Eden exists so richly in what some would call the 'collective unconscious', is it not possible that it once existed for real? If the Flood, which inevitably also has a place in this story, seems that little bit more probable to a post-tsunami, climate-changed, asteroid-watching contemporary consciousness, doesn't that suggest that it may reflect some real event. It is referred to in Genesis and the Epic of Gilgamesh. It provides a very plausible explanation for a wave of extinctions, the disappearance of vast cultures, a radical redrawing of maps that might have shown Eden and Nod in their actual attitudes and locations.

The medical argument perhaps gains a slight edge from what happened next. Though it might have been because I was heavy with food and jangled from cold nights in sleeping bags on hard mountain ground, I began to yawn and drowse. A longish stop had been planned, so there was no real reason to fear being left behind or posted missing. I picked out a spot underneath the tree, wedged my back against it, and fell asleep.

There are no dreams to recount, just a steady passage of dark in which I was conscious of water, perhaps conscious of listening for my companions, but nothing else. I wakened when something touched my outstretched foot. Standing in front of me was a girl of such awkward beauty I might have invented her. She was holding out a small basket of apricots, wrinkled as if about to collapse with their own sweetness. She gave a raw laugh as I struggled to my feet. My crossed ankles had left one foot numb and I staggered like a drunk. Her smile showed brown teeth and a couple of dark gaps. She pointed towards the door in the wall, jabbing a brown finger and then turning an imaginary steering wheel. It was time to go.

I shuffled towards the spring to throw water on my face. As I bent, a coppery shape somewhere between the texture of rough leather and fine chain mail jerked upright. I saw a gape of yellowish white and a spray of fluid hit my shirt. The smell was sharp, slightly medicinal, but the spat venom didn't touch my eyes. Backing away, I could hear the girl speaking urgently and another voice responding. Stepping over the threshold stone was an old man with a white beard. A small monkey sat on his shoulder, with a chain from its collar. It mugged furiously at me as the old man walked past. He was carrying a heavy stick. For a minute or two, he poked among the plants, tentatively and without malice, then shrugged and gave up. He and the girl looked on as I left, faces neutral and hard to read, she scratching herself, he passing up pistachio nuts to the monkey, who shelled, ate and discarded them with cartoonish despatch. Whether they were amused at my fright, offended by my trespass, or insulted because I declined those wizened fruits, I couldn't judge.

Ten minutes later, the van was moving and again we headed east.

I have been vague about location. As Fleetwood Vibe says, this geography is as much spiritual as physical and across the intervening years that drowsy garden with its simple plenitude and its fleeting moment of dis-enchantment has settled so deeply and pervasively into mind that it requires no effort of recall but, like the earliest memories of childhood, shimmers suggestively rather than offering up meaning.

Almost twenty years after that strange journey I began to read about excavations taking place at a hill site some fifteen kilometres north east of Urfa, very close to our stopping point that day. The site was called Gobekli Tepe, or the 'hill with a navel'. During the 1990s, a series of pillars, structures and carved figures were uncovered, clearly built for ritual rather than domestic function. The construction was made somewhere between 10000 and 9000 BC, a date which seemed to confound the long-held belief that no large stone buildings preceded the transition from hunting-gathering to agriculture. Somewhere around 8000 BC, a date which coincides with the first domestication of cereals, the temple at Gobekli Tepe was deliberately buried.

What else was found and what this may mean will be discussed in more detail in a later chapter. Many of the Gobekli Tepe findings, though, are enigmatic in the extreme. A carved animal seems to guard the site; no one has yet identified the species – perhaps a mountain lion, perhaps a reptile. However, there are some certainties. Radiocarbon dating makes certain its astonishing age and its association in some way with the great transition to agriculture, which in the Genesis story is bound up with Fall, banishment and fratricide; Abel was a huntsman, Cain the farmer. Most potently of all, Gobekli Tepe lies in the Fertile Crescent, between the headwaters of the rivers Tigris and Euphrates. We have always looked to their mouths for traces of our origins, but there is an alternative which squares as well, perhaps better, with the Genesis version. If that story represents an allegorical folk-memory of how our civilisation underwent its most profound evolution, then did I walk in Eden that day?

2

The serpent is a cliché, of course. So are the drowsing man under the tree, the woman offering fruit, the sense of things as yet unnamed, the sudden banishment. The old man with the monkey would be outrageous, if he were an invention. Is *this* how he intends to smuggle Darwin into the story? you might ask, but then you might just as easily return to other familiar details of the myth and wonder why the protagonist didn't waken with a dyspeptic pain below the rib, why he chose not to sample that fruit (unless dyspepsia was again the reason), why there was no mention of a second tree in the garden, why the cast remains fully clothed. We have a powerful susceptibility to the Genesis story, albeit often at an unconscious level; it is hard-wired into us – if, that is, we come from anywhere in the Judaeo-Christian orbit.

The story of Genesis, says the anthropologist Hugh Brody, is not *a* myth; it is *the* myth, whose universality is 'assumed and implicit'. Subtract Adam and Eve, the snake, the trees of life and of the knowledge of good and evil, Cain and Abel, the first murder, the flood and the ark, the rainbow, and the tower of Babel from the sum of our culture and how much is left? There are other versions, cast in Arabic and Ethiopic, and with a dramatically changed landscape of stones and sand, but Genesis is unexcelled.

It is a paradoxical story in many ways. In the first chapter, God seems effortless. Or is it that he acts as the facilitator and herald of some even larger power? God does not so much create as announce. Those who would reconcile biblical and modern cosmological thinking are pleased to believe that *Fiat Lux!* simply expresses the imminence and inevitability of the Big Bang. In the second chapter, though, God is required to get his hands dirty, so to speak. He shapes Adam out of the dust; the name and the word for earth are virtually the same in Hebrew, so we already know that man's very substance is bound up with the soil. God then plants a garden. As Brody notes – for it goes to the heart of his argument – there is a certain withdrawal here from an earlier assurance that man will have dominion over the animals. For the moment they are not part of the picture. Man lives alone in the garden with his herbs and fruits and nuts. He is responsible for tilling and sowing. With God's help he creates a helpmeet and names her Eve.

Here is where the story again turns paradoxical. In the first place, it isn't the serpent who tells the first lie, but God himself. He tells Adam and Eve that they may eat of the Tree of Life but not of the Tree of the Knowledge of Good and Evil. He tells the first couple that to eat of the second tree is death. One might say that the divine untruth is a kindly one, intended to protect his most vulnerable creations from the still worse punishment of eternal banishment, but it is a lie just the same and as such a troubling detail.

The temptation of Eve is a first demonstration of the power of language. The snake does not threaten her with his sting. His words invest the fruit with a fatal glamour; the King James version's 'good for food' is only a lame version of the original Hebrew, which identifies the fruit with raw desire. Eve uses the same method on her husband. His fall from grace happens even before his lips touch that apple or pomegranate; it happens as soon as he reaches for it, seduced by speech.

Adam and Eve do not die. They are banished from the garden, with no hope of return. Adam is again sentenced 'to till the ground from whence he was taken'. God makes it clear that this will be no easy labour; from now on, Adam must earn their living 'In the sweat of thy face'. There has so far been no mention of the world outside, but in their exile Eve gives birth to two sons. Cain and Abel are conjoined in the mind by a single act of murderous violence, but they are a puzzling pair in many ways. The fated Abel seems to take up the responsibility vouchsafed Adam and then quietly withdrawn. He is a keeper of sheep. His brother Cain tills the ground. Vegetarians and those who believe violence is somehow bound up

44

with red meat and dairy products find this bother-some. Almost everyone else forgets *why* brother kills brother, merely that it happened.

Cain and Abel make offerings to God. The elder Cain brings some of his crops; Abel sacrifices one or more (it isn't clear) of his fattest firstlings. God seems impressed by the meat and less than enthralled by Cain's basket of tubers and roots. God sees that the elder boy is not pleased with his gift's reception. *Try harder*, he seems to say, but the rest of his message is obscure, but seems to dangle a deadly temptation of its own: 'and if thou doest not well, sin lieth at the door. And unto thee shall be his desire, and thou shalt rule over him.' Cain speaks to his brother in the fields and kills him.

The first parents have by this point apparently disappeared from the story. It's Cain we follow into the land of Nod, on the east of Eden. God has cursed the land he tills, meaning that it will always be insuf-ficient for his needs. Cain will be a wanderer on the earth. We might imagine him like some American pioneer, putting down shallow roots wherever he settles, drawing them up again and moving on whenever the exhausted land fails to deliver him a subsistence. Cain, though, doesn't seem prepared to accept that fate. He has a simple, and devastatingly modern, solution. He builds a city and names it after his son Enoch. His great-great-great-grandson Lamech takes two wives. With Adah, he has Jabal, a nomadic herdsman, and Jubal, who is expert on the harp and organ. With Zillah, he has a girl Naamah, about whom nothing more is said, and a son Tubalcain, who becomes the instructor to a new class of metalworkers, 'artificer[s] in brass and iron'; these are the first industrialists. Lamech also admits to an obscure act of violence against a young man and recognises that Cain's punishment will be visited on him as well, but seven-and-seventy fold.

Even believers with a respectable knowledge of scripture hesitate if asked whether Adam and Eve had any other children. The absence of girls in the first family might be a tricky detail for literalists, but read on, they are there, unnamed sons and daughters, but also a special third son who replaced the slaughtered

Abel in the bereaved couple's hearts. He is called Seth. The chronologies and longevities are confusing at this point and so is the existence of Cain's descendant Methusael and Seth's son Methusaleh – who lives to be 969, or is that the length of his bloodline? There appear to be a second Lamech, via Seth, who at the age of 182 also has a late son. His father calls him Noah and with no obvious irony pronounces 'This same shall comfort us concerning the work and toil of our hands, because of the ground which the LORD hath cursed'. A comfort? The same Noah who discovers wine and appears before his children naked? He might have saved the whole of Creation in the days of the Flood, but Noah ended his days as another cursed husbandman and something of an embarrassment.

Nothing in Genesis is more powerful than the sense that gardening and farming are somehow the occupations of the damned. The self-replenishing richness of Eden seems the most distant of memories. The sentence on Cain and on the subsequent generations of Adam is to wander.

My obsession with the idea – and also the location – of Eden began young and has lasted a lifetime. It started, I suspect, hearing my father reciting *Paradise Lost*, which he could do at extraordinary length, but it also came from a steady blurring in his stories of a childhood place where nature and self were undivided with the inexhaustible richness of West Africa where he began his soldiering in 1943. 'Edenic' was his ultimate adjective. I imbibed his wanderlust, but also his passion for gardening, and so am settled and unsettled all at once, bequeathed with that knowledge that the ground must be manured, composted, mulched constantly because it has been cursed with insufficiency. To begin with, I preferred the theory to the practice. My favourite reading was a battered paperback compilation of gardening advice by – of course – Adam of the *Sunday Express*, a bearded Edwardian ancient whose hotbeds were architectural marvels and whose bean-rows seemed of geometrical precision. No Mrs Adam (as if her first name would ever be vouchsafed to us) was in evidence, no trouble-some under-gardener or pot-boy. Adam occupied his world all alone, and with an expression that suggested only mild effort, no sadness or loss.

Like the Manchurian candidate, I am pro-grammed to react to the word itself. I hungrily pounce on anything with 'Eden' in the title. As a child I read and re-read James Vance Marshall's *A River Ran Out Of Eden*, which isn't about Eden at all but the lives of Eskimo hunters. I graduated to John Steinbeck's *East of Eden*, though my father vastly preferred *The Grapes of Wrath*, and I proudly date my blooding in literary criticism, which became a profession later, to the moment when I recognised that the characters' initials, Charles and Adam, Cal and Aron, were a reference to Cain and Abel, and Charles's dark forehead scar a version of the mark of Cain. I felt a surge of excitement when Ernest Hemingway's strange homoerotic fantasy *The Garden of Eden* was posthumously published and, like everyone else, left it puzzled, slightly troubled, and thinking that perhaps there was a side to

Papa only the more psychologically acute of us had suspected.

I feared that Matthew Kneale might have cut across my bows with his *English Passengers*, a brilliant historical sea-yarn premised on one character's belief that the Garden of Eden lay in Tasmania, and was somewhat reassured to discover it was fiction, though of course that in no way diminishes its truth-value.

More recently, I devoured the essays in Madden's and Finch's *Eating in Eden: Food and American Utopias,* at least five words in that title that could transport me across a bookshop floor. I also admired Euan Eisenberg's encyclopaedic but still personal *The Ecology of Eden.* That ardent secularist Richard Dawkins has a propensity for dis-enchantment. There's an obvious hint of Genesis in his *Unweaving the Rainbow,* but his *River Out of Eden* made an important impact on some of the ideas I discuss in chapter five, as well as reminding me of Marshall's bittersweet 'pastoral'. And it's there as a deeply ironic metaphor in Lee M. Silver's *Remaking Eden*, a discussion of the scientific and moral challenge of cloning. I couldn't have passed on Morris

Dickstein's *Gates of Eden,* though aware it was the Bob Dylan reference which made that title so evocative. And of course, I have never stopped re-reading Hugh Brody's luminous real-life version of the Marshall novel, his luminous account of Inuit hunter-gatherers *The Other Side of Eden*, from which some of the above is unashamedly but respectfully drawn. Hanging over my study desk is the tiny woodcut by Eric Gill from *Nisi Dominus* showing Adam at his spade startled by Eve with the fruit while the serpent slides lasciviously between her thighs. On the shelf underneath a book of Lucas Cranach plates, its cover reproducing perhaps our most vivid imagining of Eden, with the Tempter revealed as human rather than herpetological. Next to that a row of books about the painter and engraver Samuel Palmer, who expresses an unfallen nature in every line. Next to those, a book of reproductions by my old friend Cecil Collins, who spent his last years in Nod and Enoch, in a tiny, split house just off the King's Road, but who insisted that the Eden he had experienced at Dartington – like Palmer's paradisal valley at Shoreham in Kent – was part of a universally shared experience, retrieved from the unconscious by art or music.

As I write, Talk Talk's abstract-pastoral *Spirit of Eden* murmurs from the speakers. Deemed 'commercially unsatisfactory' by the band's label EMI, it was my constant soundtrack through 1988, the blackest year of my life, and it still offers a gentle solace. I also have to confess a more embarrassing fondness for Iron Butterfly's preposterous 'In-A-Gadda-Da-Vida', even if only because the title is supposed to have been a mishearing of 'In the Garden of Eden'.

This is all in the realm of symbolism and iconography, but I have also obsessed about Eden as – potentially at least – a real place. I pore over gazetteers and atlases, wondering that Eden, Wisconsin, should sit just south of Mt Calvary, or that there should be an Eden Valley near Roswell in New Mexico where the alien scare of the late 1940s had its iconic moment. And I have spent much of my adult life visiting and exploring those places which hold some claim to the location of that first garden. Only one has proved inaccessible. Again as I write, the once-fertile belly of land that lies between Tigris and Euphrates stands as a living symbol of the Fall and banishment. It's hard not to see in Black Hawk 'copter blades and American armour a proliferating version of the weapon – 'a flaming sword which turned every way' – placed by God at the gate of Eden to prevent Adam and Eve from ever returning. In the absence of full credentials as a foreign correspondent, nothing would persuade the Ministry of Defence to allow a visit to Basra, and every evening's news offered consoling evidence that here was another kindly prohibition. I have to settle with the memory of a long look across for a long gaze towards the border line from the Iranian highlands, the area littered with the debris of the ayatollahs' Karbala-5 offensive of January and February 1987 to capture Basra.

What the Iranians called the *Jang-e-tahmili* or Imposed War, and which was known by Iraqis as Saddam's *Qadisiyah*, after the 7th century defeat of the Persians had ended on 20 August 1988. I visited Iraq some three months after the ceasefire, the trip again organised by Persian contacts and given a veneer of academic respectability by papers on 17th-century metaphysical poetry (much admired in Persia) and on Milton's prose (a more controversial topic, given his strictures on censorship in the great *Areopagitica*) delivered to a small group of fiercely intelligent postgraduates. That official blessing really only was veneer-thin was obvious when our drive out to the highlands was tailed unswervingly by a black jeep whose occupants were evidently communicating with contacts on the road ahead, because every fifty miles or so we'd pass another vehicle would appear by the roadside or cruise slowly past us going in the opposite direction, one of the passengers muttering darkly into a bulky cellphone or radio.

I was debriefed on my return by two more young Americans, ageless clones of those a decade earlier, but this time sharper and more insistent. As we drove from Felixstowe to London, they talked among themselves, largely ignoring me in the back, dropping the names of related US operations during the 'Tanker War' – Nimble Archer, Prime Chance, Eager Glacier, Praying Mantis, Earnest Will – as casually and gently as if they were new breeds of hybrid tea rose or race-horses in the Kentucky Derby.

What I learned on that journey was that the roots of the various Middle East conflicts were not so much historical as archaeological and biblical. The clash between Iraq (a country contrived by the Allies as a buffer zone and bulwark) and Iran (whose empire preceded the rise of the Ottoman and occupied most of modern Iraq) went back thousands of years before Christ, back even before the time of the conqueror Enmebaragesi of Kish, the first political ruler in history for whom clear archaeological evidence survives. Those ancient conflicts were essentially a land-grab for the fertile soil and mineral riches of Khuzestan, seat of the Elamite empire and of a non-Semitic, non-Indoeuropean-speaking people. Was this another candidate for Eden, I wondered, a small, walled paradise, fabled for abundance and possessed by exotic speakers who seemed to stand apart from the Babel of imperialist politics. Or was the story of Eden after all a myth spun out of nothing, a retrospective and perhaps nostalgic retelling of the human story with a common origin invented to give the curse-and-blessing of agriculture not just a dramatic spin but also a certain resolution of focus at the shimmering horizon of collective memory.

My search for Eden has been as much metaphysical as physical, the dust that surrounds it the dust of the library as well as of the road. It begins, and continues to begin always, with the name itself. So as well as asking Where was Eden? we have to ask What was Eden?

3

There is no straightforward answer in etymology. This should be no surprise, since word-origins are often as treacherous as ancient geographies, and chance resemblances or homonyms often fit misleadingly well. It's worth remembering that missed and forced readings are not unique to the analysis of biblical texts. A slew of reference books will tell you that 'utopia', a term created by Sir Thomas More in the 16th century, means 'nowhere' or 'no-place' when the Greek particle at the beginning clearly also implies 'eu-topia', 'beautiful' or 'harmonious' place as in 'euphony' or 'eurhythmics'. It should be no surprise that a name that dates to many, many hundreds of years earlier should be even more clouded and uncertain.

It is generally accepted that 'Eden' derives from the Hebrew *'eden'* which means 'delight' or 'bliss', but this by no means exhausts the possibilities. In an important 1984 essay in *Vetus Testamentum*, Alan R. Millard, emeritus professor and an honorary senior fellow at the University of Liverpool whose expertise lies in the field of Semitic languages and Babylonian flood narratives, argues that the name comes from the Semitic particle *'dn'* which denotes lushness or abundance. In Sumerian, *'eden'* means 'fertile plain'. These translations fit equally well.

There is a question about whether Eden is the name of a whole region or of a garden – real or metaphorical – within that region, and whether the word is descriptive of the garden or simply the name of a place. Genesis is relatively clear. In chapter 2:viii, the text says that 'God planted a garden, eastward in Eden', which implies that the garden is contained within a wider region that bears that name. If so, 'the Garden *in* Eden' is perhaps less ambiguous than 'the Garden *of* Eden'. This is born out by references in the Koran and the Talmud which seem to make it clear that the garden is distinct from Eden, but located within it.

'Paradise' as a synonym for Eden makes a certain etymological sense, though the term is used elsewhere in the Old Testament with no overt association and it is only in the Talmud and in certain millennialist texts from after the Exile that the terms seem to be used interchangeably. The Hebrew word, transliterated as something like *'P'rd's'*, bears a strong resemblance to the Old Persian word *'paridaida'*, later *'pairdeaza'*, which means a walled orchard or sometimes a hunting park, alternate meanings which both fit the hunting-gathering model. Intriguingly, the word also strongly resembles the Sanskrit *'paradesha'*, which means 'supreme place', though whether in a political/military sense or because of its natural grandeur and plenitude remains ambiguous. The word occurs on one or two occasions in the Old Testament and notably in the Song of Songs, where it unambiguously refers to an orchard.

'Paradise' seems most often used when Eden is projected as a destination for the blessed, like the Elysian Fields of the Greeks and Eden is often conflated in iconography with the Greek Garden of the Hesperides whose golden fruit is visible in Cranach's image of the temptation and Fall. In the Christian tradition, Paradise is the home of the blessed rather than the ancestral garden. On the cross, Jesus tells the Good Thief – known in the apocryphal Gospels as Dismas – that he will be with him in Paradise, meaning heaven. The Mormons who regard Jackson County, Missouri, as the seat of Eden also believe that Jesus will walk among them again there on the last day.

⌒

On 10 October 1988, I flew into Paradise. My host welcomed me to the 'Life of Eternity'. More prosaically, the tourist guides and business brochures refer to it as 'Two Waters' or the 'Pearl of the Persian Gulf', but Bahrain has always been regarded as one of the possible sites of Eden, and 'Paradise' is not merely a promotional metaphor.

We drove to Karrana, a sprawling village in the northern governorate of the island and one of the population centres that spraddles across the Budaiya Highway. This is the farming belt, well-irrigated and vigorous, a contrast to the unconvincing verdancy of the lawns and formal plantings in Al Manama, the capital, which are dependent on steady mists of water and nutrients, seep-pipes underground and every possible protection against evaporation. Nowadays, more than 90% of Bahrain is desert, its aquifers running dry just as oil production, begun in 1932, was reaching its peak. The 'Two Waters' may refer to the Northern and Southern stretches of the Persian Gulf, at whose mid-point Bahrain sits, or it may be a reference to the sweet springs of the island as against the acrid salt of the sea. Either way, it is hard to imagine that this was once a garden of mythical proportions, perhaps the garden that first cradled our kind.

In ancient times, Bahrain was known as Dilmon – or Telmun – and seems to have been an important entrepôt in the rich trade between Mesopotamia and the Indus Valley civilisation. Known as 'the Land of the Living', or 'the Land Where the Sun Rises', it is the apparent location of the Sumerian creation myth. Enki, the god of wisdom, water, crafts and creation, lay asleep under the sea, unable to hear the complaints of his fellow-gods, who were weary of the physical labour required to grow wheat and make bread. But the primal sea brought the salt of their tears to Enki's lips. With the help of the birth-goddess Nimma, he uses mud and clay to shape the first men, specifically as farm labourers so that the gods can enjoy their ease.

In another part of the cosmogonic myth, Dilmon is home to Sud, the queen and consort of Enlil, who controls the northern winds. He rapes her in a scented cedar forest so that she gives birth to a son Nanna, the future moon god. Enlil is punished for his violence and Sud, now renamed Ninlil, joins him in an underworld exile, where a second son is born. This is Nergal, the future god of death.

The Sumerian version is blunter than Genesis about the exact cause of the primal couple's shame, but the parallels are too powerful to miss. They are underlined by yet another alternative name for Ninlil, who is known as the demon Lilitu in one of the Gilgamesh tales. Is this the Lilith, who was Adam's first, dark consort in non-canonical versions of the creation story? Enlil certainly has another mate, the lady Aruru or Nintur, who is also known as 'the childbearer' or 'she who opens her legs'.

Dilmon suffered its own fall. Once a seething conduit for precious goods – there is no reliable record, but one has to assume they would have included valuable hardwoods, pearls, gold, ivory, lapis lazuli, copper and textiles, as well as foods and spices – the island enjoyed its golden age during the 500 years leading up to the middle of the second millennium BC. It was then that the Indus civilisation mysteriously collapsed, leaving Dilmon no longer a trade bridge between powerful civilisations but fated to sit at the fringes of empire. The Greeks knew her as Tylos; the Portuguese came in 1521, and began a slow tug-of-war with the Persian empire, who knew the islands as Mismahig. In 1783 Ahmad ibn Khalifa al Khalifa swept in from his base in neighbouring Qatar and reclaimed the Awal archipelago for his Bani Utub descendants, calling in Britain as a guarantor of independence.

My host understood these ancient histories were more than folklore. Hassan was a political scientist by training and a student of mythology by inclination. His father ran a sweet water plant not far from Karrana. He likened his country's history to a heartbeat, his hands miming the systole and diastole. Once, he said, Bahrain's territory and influence had stretched to the northern shore of the Persian Gulf and Basra. Then the inevitable decline; but then, again, new opportunities. An Oxford education notwithstanding, Hassan regarded Bahrain's years as a British protectorate with some ambivalence, but accepted that 'the Anglo-Saxons' had brought stability. Oil made the country wealthy, but precariously so, and it was only when Bahrain took over from Beirut as the Middle East's main financial centre that the scales tipped significantly. We'd driven through the financial district on the way from the airport, past rows of buildings whose mirror fronts were as blank and pitiless as the dark glasses of the security policemen who stood in every doorway.

Seven years earlier, and just a decade after the country had become an independent emirate under Isa bin Salman (the last sheikh prior to independence), there had been a Shi'a plot to overthrow the Al Khalifas and instal a theocratic government controlled by Tehran. It failed, and in doing so strengthened Bahrain's perceived status as a valuable chip in the Middle Eastern game. Hassan was a player, though his exact role at the time of the coup was strictly off the agenda. We ate dates, drank his father's bottled water, and I listened to him intone his country's history in solemn musical periods.

Did he believe Eden may have lain at Dilmon? Hassan shrugged. There were probably many Edens, he said, created in the memory of real places. He ran his hand through the stony soil at his feet. We are each of us, in our different cultures, cursed with the memory of a time when the earth seemed unstintingly bountiful and cursed with the knowledge that we now have to labour for our food and rely on others for its getting. We draw up oil from the ground – or coal, or diamonds, or yellowcake uranium – and we wound it in the process. Given that he would one day soon inherit the family plant – his father was dying, slowly and stoically, of stomach cancer – Hassan was understandably keen to argue that mankind's future, or future destruction, lay in guaranteeing supplies of water, not oil. The land behind us lay parched and inhospitable, the sea brackish with the gods' tears, the remaining inland springs jealously commercialised. Hassan had recently visited Australia and the American southwest on his father's behalf and had come back with the conviction that there, too, water would be the most pressing political issue of the 21st century.

As we stood facing the sea, a wind blew in from the water, unexpectedly sharp and with a dry taint of distant smokes. It was Enlil's wind, rude and violent. It chilled, but brought no rain, nothing to fill those dried-up watercourses that had once ripped up the wadis behind us and sweetened their banks with growth.

Genesis is very specific about the location of Eden. Contrary to any notion that the Biblical Eden is an unmappable metaphor placed vaguely 'eastward', in the dazzle of the morning sun, we are given surprisingly precise co-ordinates.

> And a river went out of Eden to water the garden; and from thence it was parted, and became into four heads. The name of the first is Pison: that is it which encompasseth the whole land of Havilah, where there is gold. And the gold of that land is good; there is bdellium and the onyx stone. And the name of the second river is Gihon. The same is it that compasseth the whole land of Ethiopia. And the name of the third river is Hiddekel. That is it which goeth toward the east of Assyria. And the fourth river is Euphrates.

Chapter and verse. But what does Genesis describe? A garden that sits in the eastern part of Eden and which is watered by a river that flows through the garden and divides into four. Some modern scholars, arguing that the story is based on folk memory and that even major details might be altered, even reversed, have suggested that the four rivers were actually tributaries of the river that flowed through Eden rather than lower branches of it. To a modern ear only one of the names in Genesis chimes with familiarity, but there is a catch even here. Place names can be deceptive. Does 'Euphrates' refer to the same river that snakes down through modern Iraq, or does the present-day river follow the same course as the ancient one? To anticipate the crux of any argument about the geography of Eden, how much remains of the antediluvian landscape in which the garden was located? Perhaps Noah and his descendants watched an unfamiliar world emerge out of the drying mud and slime and simply gave its new contours and watercourses familiar names. There is no reason to doubt that the ancient world was at some time drowned by a catastrophic flood. The

2005 tsunami, caused by the merest seismic shrug, silenced more than a few biblical non-literalists with the recognition that an even larger event, caused by a larger earthquake or by collision with an asteroid or comet, might well have seemed like the end of the world to an isolated population without a modern global perspective or mass communications. Either way, 'Euphrates' is mentioned without a gloss, as if it were substantial and central enough not to require any further detail.

Of the remaining rivers that ran out of Eden, only one can be identified with any certainty. Just as 'Hister' – object of much excitement among students of Nostradamus, who see its 'rise' as prophetic of Adolf Hitler – is actually an old name for the river Danube, so the mysterious 'Hiddekel' is merely an ancient name for the Tigris. This begins to establish parameters for Eden, and would seem to point to the most commonly favoured location in southern Iraq, or possibly under the waters of the modern Persian Gulf, which was once dry land.

That only leaves the Pison and Gihon. For

centuries, scholars argued that these must, by some unexplained logic of priority among great rivers – refer to the Nile and the Ganges. More recent experts, and notably Juris Zarins of Southwest Missouri University in Springfield, believe that the Gihon is the Karun River in western Iran, which flows south from below the Caspian Sea to the Persian Gulf, though that explanation ignores the biblical assertion that it bounds Ethiopia. That at least is easily enough explained because that geographically confusing reference in the King James Version was, like so much else in that great book, the result of a committee decision. The Hebrew text gives the area bounded by Gihon as 'Kush' or 'Gush', an old name for Ethiopia, but which may also refer to the region of Mesopotamia occupied until around a millennium before Christ by the Kashshu or Kashshites.

We learn a little more about the other river. The Pison – often Pishon – is said to bound Havilah, a name associated with the 'Sand Region' of Arabia-Felix, usually placed in the north and west of Yemen. Though it was generally known that much of the

Arabian peninsula was once fertile, until LANDSAT satellite imagery became available it was difficult to identify a candidate for Pison. The same scholars and Dr Calvin Schlabach believe that it corresponds to the now-dry Wadi Batin system.

There is, we are told by the Genesis scribe, good gold in Havilah. There is gold in Arabia about three hours drive south of Medina, at Mahd edh-Dhahab in the 'Cradle of Gold' and it is here that satellite researchers have located the buried course of a now dry river system that winds north-east towards modern Kuwait. The region underwent dramatic climatic changes in pre-history, alternating periods of wet and dry. It is generally understood that around thirty millennia BC, the Persian Gulf area was dry all the way to the Strait of Hormuz, and presumably irrigated by the river complex alluded to in Genesis. At this period in pre-history, most of Eurasia was clenched in the Great Ice Age and sea levels were much lower than at present. From around 15000 BC decreasing precipitation pushed Palaeolithic populations out of the region, east to the Indus valley, west to the shores of the Mediterranean, south west to the Nile Valley, and north into the so-called 'Fertile Crescent' bounded by the Tigris and Euphrates. Then, around 5000 BC, the rains returned in what is known as the Neolithic Wet Phase and populations returned to the Arabian peninsula and surrounding regions, attracted by what must have seemed a paradisal abundance. The difference now was that human populations were growing exponentially and in place of the old hunting and foraging, agriculture was evolving, with all the ambiguities that brought in its wake. All cultural evolutions move with what seems in proper hindsight to be geological slowness. This might be an exception. Though palaeontologists and historians insist that the transition to agriculture was a process rather than a dramatic event, it seems to have had the emotional impact of the latter, easily comparable to the psychological disturbance and sense of loss described at the time of Enclosure in England, the Industrial Revolution, and current in the Silicon Revolution. All stories of Eden have an elegiac, literally nostalgic cast, a recognition that the simple plenitude of the old ways had given way to something that required organisation, hierarchies of skill and opportunity, conflict and an immitigable sense of loss.

In addition to gold, other precious commodities are mentioned. Onyx stone may refer to lapis lazuli, but there is a measure of uncertainty about bdellium. It is mentioned once more in the Bible, when in Numbers the manna that sustained the Children of Israel in the desert is likened to coriander seed and in colour to bdellium, or *bedolach* in Hebrew. The substance seems to be a kind of rich gum, similar to myrrh but cheaper and more plentiful and so used as an adulterant. Most researchers believe it refers to the tapped sap of the guggul or Mukal myrrh tree (*Commiphora wrightii*), common in northern India and an important specific in Ayurvedic medicine, where it is used to treat anything from arthritis to epilepsy; it has the additional value of balancing cholesterol and dealing with problems associated with obesity – which adds a thoroughly modern resonance to an ancient remedy.

I saw such a tree in a garden just outside Sana'a, which in 1988 was the capital of the Yemen Arab Republic, or North Yemen, soon to be unified with its Marxist southern neighbour. Relations between the two Yemens had been surprisingly cordial despite their ideological differences. The border – unlike the bristling 'demilitarised' zone dividing North and South Korea – was effectively undefined and passage back and forth was relatively easy. But not for a young Westerner. I had hoped to travel to Aden. The Arabic name for Eden, *jannato aden,* sounded like nothing more than another philological *faux ami,* a coincidental resemblance, but this was a journey that might just as well be conducted on the principle of serendipity. My two closest friends at school, twins, were the sons of a former harbour master at Aden and had lived there during the Emergency when the Argyll and Sutherland Highlanders under the command of Lt Col Colin Mitchell had policed the territory against the insurgents of the National Liberation Front and of the Front for the Liberation of Occupied South Yemen (what irony of history threw 'Mad Mitch' up against something as deceptively mild-sounding as 'FLOSY'?). They had left well before the final British withdrawal in 1967, so I grew up with stories of primed grenades wedged into sprung cinema seats and of cowboy shootouts where the bad guys wore Arab headdresses instead of black hats and the good guys were in chequered glengarries. In the Mid-East, the rules of engagement were strictly Wild West, and I thrilled to that.

Later, there was another reason to obsess about Aden. It was from there in 1880 that a 26-year-old French poet turned merchant and gun-runner with the mark of Cain on him had written home to his family with an image as far removed from Paradise as can be imagined. Abandoning verse, Arthur Rimbaud had gone in search of an undifferentiated sensuality beyond language and far from the stiff chills and thin gruels of northern France. He went to Arabia-Felix to breathe in the musk of coffee, spice, rich resins and *Boswellia* gums, frankincense and myrrh, perhaps guggul and benjamin, but experienced instead a whiff of the pit.

There isn't a single tree, not even a
withered one, not a single blade of grass,
patch of earth or drop of fresh water. Aden
is the crater of an extinct volcano, the
bottom of which is filled with sea-sand.
There's absolutely nothing to see or touch
except lava and sand which are incapable of
producing the tiniest scrap of vegetation.
The environs are an absolutely arid desert
of sand.

If this was not 'a season in hell', it's hard to understand what might have been.

⮌

I flew to Sana'a from Bahrain, with a small packet of
rials and a letter of introduction from Hassan's father
to Dr Omar Sidiqi, a passionate amateur of Rimbaud's
work whose great-great-grandfather claimed to
have met and known the poet in the forbidden city
of Harar in Ethiopia. Rimbaud had first travelled

there in 1880, against all advice and unaware that the young French explorer Henri Lucereau had been killed there by Itou tribesmen shortly before. Until 1855, Harar had been unvisited by Westerners and was only precariously opened up by Richard Burton's daring sortie into the Abyssinian interior. Rimbaud returned twice more, in 1883 and 1888. He left not long before his death in 1891, already suffering from the cancerous growth – diagnosed on his return to France as a *neoplasme de cuisse* – that would cost him his right leg and ultimately his life, still dreaming of a return to Aden and of escape from a France that had just rediscovered the 'missing' *poete maudit*.

Sidiqi met me at his door with the laconic comment 'Ah, you have Rimbaud's blue eyes. But not his physique, I think'. In place of a handshake, he ran his fingers over my upper arms and shoulders, like a farmer assessing a sale bullock. He was short himself and slight, with a dip to his walk that seemed to be caused by a withered leg, but he moved with a curious, asymmetrical grace. At home, he wore Western clothes, light cotton trousers and shirt, ancient sandals on his feet. I noticed that he wore a gold ring with a lapis setting on his right middle finger. There was a scent in his study, equal parts bitter and sweet and built on a base of moulded paper and decaying leather. I found wormholes in some of his books, the open pages letting down a light dandruff of debris.

We talked about William Blake and about my Edinburgh friend Reza Sabri-Tabrizi's Marxist interpretation of his *Heaven and Hell*. There were interruptions as members of Sidiqi's staff brought in papers. He glanced at them and either nodded or shook his head. Nothing was signed. I asked what his business was, but there was no reply. Once, prompted by a thought, he rose, and pulled an unostentatious *djellabiyah* over his head and disappeared into another part of the house. There were voices, hard to read as to mood or temper, and while he was gone one of the staff came to the doorway and looked at me, but Sidiqi offered no explanation of his absence.

Later, someone brought coffee, the very commodity – along with ivory – that had lured Rimbaud to Harar and beyond. Did he know the tradition that Rimbaud had written a book about Abyssinia and that it had been left behind or lost during his pained portage back to the coast? Yes, Sidiqi said, his revered grandfather – the white head nodded respectfully and called down a blessing – had seen it, passed down through the family, but its whereabouts were no longer known. There was, however, a photograph.

He led me into the corridor outside the study. In a small niche, a creased sepia print stood propped against the stone, unframed and apparently disregarded. It might have been a white man, might even have been Rimbaud, but the surface of the plate had been so spotted with moulds and damp that it was only possible to identify a human figure. What struck me was the subject's awkward pose, both arms up in front of the chest as if carrying some invisible weight. It reminded me perversely of the infamous 'faked' photograph of Lee Harvey Oswald, holding his cheap rifle and an eclectic spread of Marxist publications.

Sidiqi let me take it out and into the light. I laid the fragile card on a table and took a photograph.

What came out when I developed it on returning home was a bizarre palimpsest, every mark and flaw on the original amplified and with an unseen flare all but eliminating the face and head. The image sat on various desks for several years and then disappeared, as thoroughly as that legendary Abyssinian manuscript.

⁓

Present-day Harar is a tourist destination, reached with some ease and in comfort, and perched in the cooler Ethiopian highlands about 500 miles from Addis Ababa. It is a place that still bustles with trade and some signs of modernity, but when Rimbaud first approached it the Forbidden City would have seemed no more than a dull blob of pinkish stone, surrounded by the *jogal* or encircling wall whose five gates represent the Five Pillars of Islam. From a distance, its undistinguished profile would have been headed by two nondescript minarets. Around its base a few hopeful gardens where fruit and sorghum were grown, when drought hadn't killed the topsoil. In 1988, almost a hundred years after Rimbaud's just four years after the disastrous famine and the ostensibly secret 'Operation Moses' that saw the repatriation to Israel of some 8000 Ethiopian Jews, Harar was a tense and chastened place. Rimbaud had been replaced by Rambo. CIA-backed actions with additional funding from Jewish-American organisations – who had foolishly leaked news of the 1984 operation – were still taking place. The biblical names – Operations Joshua and Solomon – were somehow appropriate in the world's second oldest Christian civilisation, but ironic too.

The King James translation of Genesis mentions Ethiopia, as we have seen, reinforcing the notion that the river Gihon may be the Nile. The country is certainly identified as one of the 'Cradles of Mankind' and the proximity of the Rift Valley, with its rich fossil record and a general consensus that this is where the first modern humans flourished, makes it another contender for the location of Eden. the very proliferation of possibilities is, of course, evidence for the idea that 'Eden' refers to a folk-memory, common to all the ancient civilisations and extrapolated from experience in different locations throughout the Fertile Crescent and the once-rich lands that surround it.

It is a land over which empires have trodden and re-trodden: from the Egyptians in ancient times to the Italians in the late 19th and 20th centuries, a colonisation that road-tested some of the worst barbarities of modern warfare, but also inspired the proud resistance of Haile Selassie, Ras Tafari Makkonen, Lion of Judah, Might of the Trinity. When Rimbaud was in Ethiopia, the ruler was the modernising Menilek II, who gave the Italians a soon-to-be-avenged bloody nose at Adowa in 1896. His name was an echo of the first ruler Menilek I, by legend the son of Solomon and the Queen of Sheba, who around 300 BC established the kingdom of Aksum. The Empire of Christ arrived in the 4th century AD, and within 200 years had adopted as dogma the Monophysite heresy that insists Christ is of single, divine nature rather than both human and divine, a belief condemned in 451 at the fourth ecumenical council at Chalcedon, now Kaldikoy in Turkey.

No one seems quite to agree when Harar was founded. Estimates range from the 7th to the 12th centuries AD, but its golden age was in the 16th when Ahmad ibn Ibrahim al-Ghazi, otherwise known as Gragn the Left-Handed, mounted a series of conquests that consolidated a Muslim kingdom and threatened the Christian Ethiopian empire. The Jamia mosque dates from that time, though today there are more than a hundred in the city, as well as the Medha Alame cathedral. They will show you the house where Rimbaud lived, and Haile Selassie, but the most notorious entertainment is the 'hyena men' who feed the prowling dogs for anyone who cares to pay them for the grisly sight.

The Harari call themselves the 'People of the City' and speak a unique Semitic dialect, originally written in Arabic script. It's sometimes known as *A'dare* and is an offshoot of the classical *Ge'ez*, which forms the basis of modern Amharic, the official language. Entering Harar, though, still seems, as it must have seemed to Rimbaud, like entering into a distinct, almost imaginary space in which the normal

83

trajectories of time are suspended. There is a modern agricultural college on the road from Dire Diwa, and a military school in the city itself, but for the most part it seems to hark back to a place and time before either farming or warfare were human imperatives. Food seemed almost plentiful, but in haphazard quantities and perhaps mindful that local names would mean nothing to my Yemeni fellow-traveller and translator, Sidiqi's nephew, the stall holders seemed disinclined to apply a name to anything.

It reminded me forcibly of that garden in south eastern Turkey: the same sense of things not named, of a precarious plenitude gained without apparent effort, a strange mixture of aggressive *laissez-faire* and drowsing passivity. No one thinks to search for Eden in the mountains. In our imaginations, it somehow logically sits in the belly-lands of rivers, but perhaps this is to mistake the nature of early human habitation. Perhaps here there was a hint that the paradigm and the iconography might be misleading.

I knew that Rimbaud had made sorties out of Harar, sometimes dressed as an Arab in red blanket

and headdress, seemingly as interested in pure explo-
ration as he was in trade. I also knew that some of his
journeying, marked by silences in his correspondence
home, had been towards the Rift Valley. If there were
a place where the palaeontological record and the
biblical story almost coincided, it was surely there, and
I sensed its nearness and its power radiating through
that dry air. Harar had the mystery and the evanes-
cent quality of a very ancient place and one which,
even though it had been caught up like the rest of the
country in a superpower-sponsored struggle for East
Africa's soul, seemed somehow occluded from modern
history. It both was and wasn't the kind of place I was
searching for.

⌐

Sidiqi had helped to arrange the trip, and at shortest
notice, because one of his nephews had some business
there. It was, he said, business that could only be
transacted in person. I had the sense of having turned
into nothing more than a querying cipher travelling

along interconnected filaments of trade like the pulse that activates a ringing phone. It seemed curiously will-less and unstructured, as if in the process of circling in on what Eden means in our deep unconscious, I was myself making the transition back from the orderly sowings and plantings of 'research' towards something like hunting-gathering. I sniped opportunistically at ideas, chased unsuspected quarry, seemed to have entered a way of living that had rendered borders and boundaries irrelevant.

I couldn't tell whether Sidiqi liked me or simply tolerated me, but he was a literary man, wise and cosmopolitan, whose own journeys seemed increasingly to be those of the mind. He enjoyed talk above all else. On the evening before I left, drinking coffee which I cheerfully imagined to be from Harar he took me outside to the garden that could be glimpsed through the narrow window pierced in his study wall. A hoopoe rose from a patch of sunlight and flapped up and over the wall like a small pinkish kite pulled by a child. Sidiqi laughed when I told him that its taxonomic name was *Upopa epops epops.* He liked the music of that. We talked about Attar's great Sufi epic *The Conference of the Birds,* where the wise Hoopoe acts as chorus, chairman and *consigliori* to the gathered fowl, and I was able to recall enough of what the poem said about Adam and his dream, and about Eblis or Satan, to impress him. We had been talking again about Genesis. He pointed to a small tree with papery bark which grew out of a rocky bed in the centre of the garden. Nearby, a tiny freshet of water snaked through a channel of rough white stones, disappearing into a terracotta pipe that cut through a small grassy mound and emerging again on the other side. Sidiqui rubbed the sparse leaves of the tree and bid me sniff the sap. This, he said, is the plant that gives bdellium, the tree that is mentioned in Genesis. And then, unexpectedly, and in the same conversational cadence my father had always used for poetry, which he believed should always be a heightened version of common speech, he recited the lines from Book IV of *Paradise Lost*, where Milton describes Eden:

Southward through Eden went a river large,

Nor changed his course, but through the shaggy
  hill
Passed underneath ingulfed, for God had
  thrown
That mountain as his garden mould high raised
Upon the rapid current, which through veins
Of porous earth with kindly thirst up drawn
Rose a fresh fountain, and with many a rill
Watered the garden …

I had often asked my father how big Eden was, and
had never had a satisfactory answer. Later, it seemed
to be less of an issue, but whenever I read *Paradise
Lost* and come to the description of Eden, as seen by
Satan in his guise of cormorant, the same curious
slippage of scale occurs. The vocabulary of the passage
– 'steep wilderness', 'grotesque and wild', 'insuper-
able height', 'stateliest view' – suggests something
larger than a walled garden.

There had been a tension throughout my
obsession with the idea and the location of Eden. Was
the garden *in* Eden? Or was Eden itself the garden?

Did it refer to a small and contained area – however often repeated throughout the collective memory of the Fertile Crescent – or did it refer instead to a whole region? Perhaps, too, our natural disposition to regard it as somewhere lush and fecund, bursting with provender, might be overdetermined by too much medieval painting. Perhaps Eden also partook of Milton's dust and heat.

4

The Puritans distrusted show, respected plainness. Any suggestion that God's Creation could be improved upon was treated with suspicion and disapproval. Something of the same spirit exists in Islam, where craftsmen will humanise a design with deliberate flaws or errors, and where gardeners favour at least an appearance of naturalness. Sidiqi's garden was a contrived wilderness, an artfully haphazard and natural scatter of trees, shrubs and herbs. One of the unseen consequences of the English Civil War was the destruction of some of the great Tudor gardens, whose complex, often geometrical designs and ostentatious plantings were grubbed up by Cromwell's soldiers. It was by no means a unique act of cultural vandalism, and it may well have been that many of those great gardens would have simply fallen victim to the vagaries of fashion in garden design, an area of creative endeavour where changes in the philosophical hegemony are translated into practice much more quickly than in other forms and disciplines. Hence, the Augustan garden, the Romantic garden, the 'wild' garden.

Teaching Milton to Iranian postgraduates was always going to be a delicate balancing act. My intention was to concentrate on the poet's prose, and in particular his great track against censorship, the *Areopagitica* of 1644. I had hopes as well of looking at the divorce tracts, in which Milton proves to be a powerful arguer and advocate of humane provision. These texts would inevitably require a circumspect approach. I had been warned that every group of students would include one spy or informer, and to that degree not so very different from any similar gathering of scholars, political radicals or merely friends in Milton's own day, when the spy rings of Elizabethan and Jacobean politics simply acquired new – and often theological – areas of 'interest'.

I had casually asked some of the students if they knew or had heard of either Kourosh or Sattar, my old friend and my mysterious 'package'. The names were common enough, they said. The following day one of the university administrators approached at the seminar room door and asked if he could be of assistance. Was there a specific reason why I was looking for these men? No, I said, *un ami de college, simplement* – French was our *lingua franca* – and the other a mere acquaintance. The names were not familiar to him, he said, but he would make enquiries if I wished. I begged him not to take any trouble and he smiled and turned to go. As I picked up my briefcase to enter the classroom, he reappeared at my elbow. It appeared that during a previous class I had mentioned the work of Reza Baraheni, the exiled Azeri poet and novelist, author of *The Crowned Cannibals*, and former professor at the University of Tehran. He had been expelled and denied the right to work some five years earlier, faring no better under the new *velayat-e fagih* (stewardship of clerical authority) than he had under the Shah and at the hands of the old regime's SAVAK secret police.

This time the university man did not meet my eye and his smile was decidedly forced. This was, perhaps, not an appropriate subject for discussion, and not relevant to my subject. I opened my mouth to explain the relevance, and closed it again.

Milton was diffident about his prose writing, suggesting that it was work of the 'left hand' rather than the real expression of his vision. Nevertheless, some of his most work can be found in the essays. His sense of the moral life as a field of effort rather than a passive state of grace is firmly restated in the *Areopagitica*, lines that that have always moved and inspired me:

> I cannot praise a fugitive and cloistered
> virtue, unexercised and unbreathed that
> never sallies out and sees her adversary but
> slinks out of the race, where that immortal
> garland is to be run for, not without dust
> and heat. Assuredly we bring not innocence
> into the world, we bring impurity much
> rather; that which purifies us is trial and
> trial is by what is contrary.

Elsewhere in the essay, he puts the same thought into the context of Eden:

> It was from out the rind of one apple tasted
> that the knowledge of good and evil as two
> twins cleaving together leaped forth into
> the world. And perhaps this is that doom
> that Adam fell into of knowing good and
> evil, that is to say, of knowing good by evil.

Though it had not been our intention to look at *Paradise Lost,* the connections seemed too strong to ignore and over the next tense and faintly paranoid days, I re-read Milton's great poem.

∽

Tabriz is known in Iran as the City of Firsts. Sitting as it does in the northwestern corner of the country, at the mountainous base of a stubby finger of territory bounded in turn by the Caspian Sea, Azerbaijan, Armenia and Iraq, and sitting sufficiently far from the capital to be able to quietly ignore the central authority when occasion suits, the 'Chocolate City' prides itself on an impressive roster of social and cultural innovations. It was the first Iranian city to install a telephone system, to found public libraries, theatre groups and a movie house, to mint coins, and to provide kindergartens as well as schools for deaf and blind children. It also boasts an impressive roster of famous sons and daughters, including several prime ministers, the children's writer Samad Behrangi, the poet and politician Jalaalolmamalek or Iraj Mirza, the beautiful singer Googoosh and, of course, the trouble-some Reza Baraheni.

But perhaps Tabriz's proud record in coming first and producing distinguished sons and daughters extends even further back in time than the days when, as 'Ta-e Vrezh' or 'This is revenge', it was a valuable counter in the to-and-fro of ancient empires. According to one theory, the steppe or plain south of Tabriz known in Akkadian as 'Edin' was where mankind first made that crucial movement from bestowal to husbandry.

It might seem strange in this context to cite the authority of an ex-rock musician, but David Rohl (formerly of Mandalaband) has devoted much of his life to a rich vein of historical enquiry. 'Egyptology' attracts as many amateurs (like Adam Harding, who we'll meet later), eccentrics and imaginative frauds as it does genuine scholars, but Rohl is a serious man, who doesn't merely juggle etymologies but does the fieldwork as well. His rigorous research on pharaonic chronology has led to a substantial revision of that murky timeline and one that substantially recalibrates the Egyptian story with the biblical narrative. It is Rohl's contention that Eden was the large open plain north and west of Mt Sahand, in a region now bounded by Lake Urmia, the Caspian Sea and, to the south, Kurdistan.

Despite his devotion to investigation *in situ* and an estimable suspicion of what might be chance philological coincidences, Rohl took some of his ideas from the work of a man who never set foot in Iranian Azerbaijan. A relatively obscure scholar called Reginald Walker had worked, as other had before him, on the problem of the four rivers that bounded Eden. As with other proposed locations for Eden, the Tigris (Hiddekel) and Euphrates represent no problem, but what again of the Gihon and Pishon. Walker discovered that the river that runs north-east from the plain of Edin to the Caspian was once known as the Gaihun and that it was referred to in 19th century gazetteers as the Gihon-Aras. This would point to a similarly coursed river to the south as the Pishon. The only candidate here is the Uizon, which seems not to fit. Here is Walker's one sleight-of-hand. Easy, he said. Pishon is merely a phonetic corruption of the original name, not hard to imagine given the liquidity of ancient vowels and consonants.

More remarkably still, Walker discovered on an old map a village called Noqdi. The final particle identifies the place as being 'of Noqd'. Could this not be the 'land of Nod, which is east of Eden'? For Walker, and subsequently for Rohl, the case seemed irresistible. It delivers an utterly convincing topography for the supposedly mythological Eden, bounded by high 'walls', the mountain ranges that cup it north, south and west and by the dingy marshlands to the east, where Cain was exiled.

Any attempt to clinch the Eden story stands or falls less on its creation than on its eventual destruction. Rohl proposes that the Flood was a local phenomenon, that the 'mountains' which were covered by the deluge were not the great ranges surrounding Edin but the small hillocks that punctuate the region and which could easily have been covered during a Neolithic Wet Phase. Rohl also deftly moves the Ark's final resting place from Mt Ararat to Mt Judi Dagh, south rather than north of Lake Van.

~

I knew nothing of Rohl and his ideas when I visited Tabriz in 1988. His book about the location of Eden, *Legend: The Genesis of Civilisation,* was not published for another ten years. I cannot claim to have anticipated his idea and marvel at the thoroughness of his research. It is an enjoyable book, which carefully tracks the syncretism between ancient Sumerian records and the biblical narrative. It's written with verve and unflappable conviction. My journey to Tabriz, by car from Tehran and in a vehicle whose exhaust seemed to be piped directly into the ventilation system, filling the interior with a grey hydrocarbon tang, was hot, long and for the most part dull, the road punctuated by anonymous cement plants. Tabriz itself was no less polluted. The Englishman who travelled with us, a postdoctoral student in a scientific discipline I never quite managed to pin down but which seemed to have something to do with polymers, commented sourly that it seemed strange that a people who produced so much oil should use such low-grade petroleum themselves.

The Citadel and Blue Mosque are both earthquake survivors, but much of the city is recent, the architecture generic. The City Hall, built in the mid-1930s by German engineers, looked as if it might well have come from one of Albert Speer's abandoned notebooks, a hulking monolith that carried only the faintest tinge of the ochre red that somehow defines the region, recalled in Adam's name, which is derived from 'red earth'.

We drank tea and ate chocolate, enough on top of the morning's intake of carbon monoxide to leave me with a dull headache, not quite a migraine but certainly in that family. After lunch, the Englishman and I persuaded our driver to take us out of the city for an hour. We drove through sprawling industrial quarters, petrochemicals and heavy plant in the main, along roads that seemed to have been recently treated with hot tar and stone chips, which meant that the windows could not be opened, and then out into open country. The relatively small traffic of cars and vans thinned further and suddenly most of the vehicles we passed were farmer's carts, which mostly seemed to be piled with thick straw and maize stalks. Children waved to us, but most of their adults who stopped and turned simply looked at the car and its occupants with neutral eyes.

Our driver was anxious to return to the city, where we were spending the night at a Technical School. As we drove back, we saw many men at evening prayers, turning from work for a moment to make their devotions where they stood, or rather knelt, symbolically washing their faces of the field dust. As we arrived in town, men from the factories were walking slowly through the streets, laughing or disputing fiercely, but with the same directness and simplicity that has always seemed to me to define the Persians.

For one poet, Tabriz was the 'neighbourhood of the beloved', and it came to me with great force that what characterised this culture most powerfully was an adhesive passion expressed in physical closeness; no sense of 'personal' space on the streets, arguments conducted with grabbed wrists, pushes and sometimes knocked heads. Family groups seemed precisely that, entities larger than their individual components. The essential movement here is centripetal rather than centrifugal, as if might be in the west and in the Anglo-Saxon world in particular. In Persian love poetry, the amatory passions are curiously undifferentiated. Somewhat as in C P Cavafy's Greek verse, or – a rare example from the English-speaking world – Hart Crane's 'Voyages', it hardly seems to matter whether the beloved addressed is male, female or partakes of both. The expressions of love are more of surrender than of conquest, but at the same time something is retained, kept close to the heart and home. Here, perhaps, is the faintest, most fugitive echo of the time when mankind huddled in neighbouring family bands, held together by need and security, kept apart – and far apart by our urban standard – by the simple territoriality of need.

If our moral divisions, like our fateful division into self-aware and sometimes uncomprehending sexes came out the rind of one apple tested, then here, perhaps, was paradise lost in its most literal form, its innate sense of struggle and its relentless dichotomies all the sharper for the physical closeness to the sources of our greatest mythology. I had no inkling of Eden, there in Iranian Azerbaijan, because what I was seeing was post-lapsarian society in its most vivid form, men and women sharply divided by custom and taboo, labour hard and unforgiving, even in a land whose fertility could almost be smelt in the soil, as soon, that is, as one got far enough away from factory chimneys and retorts. It was and is, though, also a land that for all its mystifying violence and curious mix of aesthetic sophistication and extraordinary vulgarity, for all its neglect of Milton's strictures against censorship, did seem to live its philosophy out in the air and streets, to avoid that 'fugitive and cloistered virtue, unexercised and unbreathed'. I gained and retain the highest respect for Shia Islam on that visit, and continually lament the perversions and political manipulations of two common-rooted scriptural traditions that have set them one against the other.

Late that evening, I walked around for a time with my companions, and examined killims and rugs being sold by vendors on a long street that seemed geared to a tourist influx that had failed to show up. With that academic instinct that prefers the analytical detail to appreciation of the whole, and seems to find in detecting fault a more worthwhile task than simple pleasure in the whole, I found myself looking in every piece for the deliberate mistake that would reveal it as a human creation and not in any sense a bid to rival the Creation. It was an odd and curiously disillusioning moment and one that perhaps marked the end, not of my interest in literary criticism or professional dependence on it, but certainly in any pleasure to be taken from its methods.

Later still, tired but agitated, and smoking restlessly, I walked again in 'paradise', in one of the walled gardens – *pairideaza* – that neighboured the Technical School. I walked without grace this time, and with no sense of closeness to Eden. The reasons were perhaps personal, but also consistent with what was, for all my pontifications on Milton and time, a false sense of what Eden actually meant. The clues are there in *Paradise Lost*. They are there in the title. Eden is not a place, but a process, and the process is defined by loss.

Adam and Eve both existed. This is scientific fact. What makes it difficult to grasp and less than satisfactory to biblical literalists is that they lived thousands of years apart and, by definition, never met. Like cosmology and particle physics, genetic research increasingly yields results that seem to confirm the essential, deep-structural truth of the most ancient mythologies. Or, perhaps more cynically, science has learned the publicity value of re-animating and hijacking mythologies that science itself had long consigned to the realm of illusion and superstition. Hence a plethora of popular science books and documentaries with names like *The Seven Daughters of Eve*, Oxford professor Brian Sykes's fine account of our genetic ancestry, or that arch-unbeliever Richard

Dawkins's *River Out Of Eden*. Their conclusions are always more carefully mediated, perhaps less emotionally satisfying than the media headlines might promise but they do provide a certain common ground.

~

Eve existed, and for seven strange, rapt days, I walked where she had walked some 140,000 years ago. There is a virtual consensus that modern humans first evolved in eastern Africa, somewhere in the territory bounded by modern Ethiopia, Tanzania and Kenya, less consensus as to how and when human populations began to colonise the rest of the planet. Some researchers argue that the emergence of *Homo sapiens* was an example of simultaneous evolution, or perhaps of several pulses of fresh evolutionary development and diffusion from the Rift Valley region. This, of course, squares rather comfortably with the possibility that the Nile is one of the four rivers mentioned in Genesis.

The paradox of what scientists call 'African Eve' – she has another, uglier name, as we'll see – is that the human story does not begin with her. The fossil record at Oldupai Gorge in northern Tanzania reveals tool-making ancestors from as far back as 2.6 million years, the creators of the so-called Oldowan artefacts now on display at the Olduvai Gorge Museum. It is the most visible relic of the work begun in the 1950s by Louis and Mary Leakey, but continued by their family and students to this day. The confusion in naming is often explained by the suggestion that 'oldupai', the Masai name for a kind of wild sisal that grows in the region, was mis-heard by the first white settlers, who then transcribed and perpetuated.

Oldupai is a steep ravine, scattered with scrub. It was once on the shores of a large lake but this eastern corner of the Serengeti is now arid. There are many strata of fossil remains. The deepest offer evidence of early hominids such as *Homo habilis* and *Paranthropus boisei*. Later deposits in Bed II show evidence for a huge technological leap forward in the carefully shaped tools of *Homo erectus*. There is evidence, too,

107

of populations of Neanderthal, those mysterious and seriously underestimated creatures who have been consigned to the preterite of human history. The upper, and thus more modern, levels show signs of a thriving industry. These are named Masek, Ndutu and Naisiusiu, and date from between 600,000 years ago and a mere 15,000. Somewhere in the middle of the period that created the Ndutu deposits, Eve walked, perhaps hunted or fished, and maybe gathered sisal or berries. We only know for certain of one thing that she did, and that is that she bore children.

A small group of Masai women peered at me as I hopefully turned over stones in the upper reaches of the gorge, their expressions neither friendly nor hostile, but too engaged to be neutral either. There were children with them who shouted when my back was turned and fell silent when I turned to smile at them. Their excitement was explained when I walked over. A large snake lay stretched out on the group, as thick as my upper arm and dismayingly long. The head had been smashed with sticks or rocks and the exposed flesh and integument was covered with brawling flies.

The corpse already smelt strongly. The women seemed to take my grin for foolish bravado. If this was a black mamba, it was the same feared species my father had told me could overtake a man on a horse and kill both. That was a curious example of a story actually *dis*-believed in childhood which I found out later to be true. But that wasn't the reason for my smile. Its main component was irony, for here again was a serpent in Eden, but this time defeated by woman.

∽

The fossil evidence is important, but contemporary science has even more powerful magic at its disposal. Or perhaps anti-magic, since the techniques of genetics seem to yield a kind of statistical dis-enchantment, as well as a thoroughly unromantic terminology. Instead of 'African Eve', meet 'mt-MRCA'. To be fair, some prefer to retain some reference to the First Mother of Us All and call her 'Mitochondrial Eve', but her more formal designation is 'matrilineal most recent common ancestor'.

The dis-enchantment doesn't stop there, for it's important to tease out those words very carefully indeed. This ancient creature, in whose legacy we all have a tiny stake thanks to our mothers and their mothers, shouldn't be seen as part of a First Couple, nor confused with an unqualified Most Recent Common Ancestor, nor does she have anything to do with the well-attested theory of population bottleneck, which posits a catastrophe situation so devastating that all later populations – of whatever species – descend from a drastically reduced pool of potential parents. Such a catastrophe seems to have overtaken mankind some 70,000 years ago when a global event – thought to the eruption of the Toba supervolcano in Indonesia and the massive climatic change that followed it – reduced the entire human population of the planet to that of a small English village, perhaps some 1000 souls. The story of the Ark acquires a little more real-world buoyancy.

If not as ancient or as primal as the biblical Eve, Mitochondrial Eve is certainly more ancient than the Most Recent Common Ancestor of all humans, who is estimated to have lived only some three millennia ago. Nor should she be thought to have been a solitary female from whom all subsequent humanity emerged. Mitochondrial Eve and her biological partner lived in a small but mixed population, but by some unexplained concatenation of evolutionary factors she was the only female to have passed on her mitochondria to subsequent generations, or to put it a better way, the mitochondria of all other living females gradually and again unexplainably died out.

It is always around this point in any such discussion that some listeners develop blank looks, so it is perhaps necessary to pause and backtrack a little. For a start, the existence of Mitochondrial Eve is a hypothesis, a very strongly plausible hypothesis, but one that some would argue is based on faulty statistical analysis. In an argument that runs parallel with that about the hypothesised Last Universal Ancestor (LUA), the organism from which all subsequent organisms have evolved, there is a suggestion that instead of a single LUA, there was a small community of like or compatible organisms from which all subsequent ones evolved. From a certain point of view, this is a more satisfactory model for the 'mt-MRCA'. Many experts accept the basic premise of Mitochondrial Eve, but argue with the 'Out of Africa' theory of human diffusion. Still others are perturbed by the biblical metaphor, which grew out of an article published in *Nature* magazine by three scientists, R. L. Cann, M. Stoneking and A. C. Wilson, and which demonstrates both the enormous media potential and the profound dangers of metaphor in scientific writing. In the wake of their article, newspapers and television programmes excitedly announced that Eve had been discovered! It seemed only a matter of time before the Garden of Eden was no more lost to us than the Lost Gardens of Heligan, which sit pleasingly close to the Eden Project in Cornwall.

The majority of blank looks, though, are prompted by the basic science behind these ideas and by a proliferation of unfamiliar terms – genetic drift, haplotypes and haplogroups, and, crucially, mitochondria themselves. Surely all organisms, and humans most obviously from our point of view, inherit DNA from *both* parents? Isn't that on page one of Genetics 101, and the basis for those striking physical similarities, red-haired, green-eyed girls and their mothers and aunts, that always strike 'outsider' in-laws at family gatherings, for the moment complacently ignoring the probability that they will pass on big noses or big feet by exactly the same process? Or for those dominant and persistent traits like the notorious 'Habsburg lip', which pouts out of countless royal portraits down the generations, or these days more commonly pursed in irritation at the thought that all a thousand years of careful breeding has bequeathed is a funny mouth and not a crown? The short answer to both is yes. Humans have 46 chromosomes (Adam seems momentarily overlooked in this narrative, but we'll be renewing acquaintance with him in this exact context very shortly) which pass on recombined traits from both parents: so, watch out for red-haired girls with big feet.

Genetic inheritance of this sort is transmitted by the nuclei of the parents' cells, which provide different components of the new generation's DNA.

There are, however, other forms of DNA and they are found in the mitochondria which provide fuel for the developing nuclei. Male and female children both have mitochondrial DNA, which is identical to the mother's, but only daughters are able to pass it on. Also, because unlike nuclear DNA this mitochondrial code is not recombined with any other, it passes on unchanged. Here's where the maths kicks in. To discover Mitochondrial Eve one simply (!) draws a diagram of everyone currently alive, and then traces the lineage back through mothers, grandmothers, great-grandmothers, great-great-grandmothers, and so on. Common-sense logic dictates that this is an infinite regress that will yield a vastly complex family tree. But because this model only takes account of matri-lineal descent, every time one encounters two women with the same mother (and therefore identical mito-chondrial DNA) the lines of descent converge rather than branching. Carry that process ever backward and by definition you come across the woman who passed on her mitochondrial DNA to every living human on the planet.

Run the model forward and it works exactly the same way. Again, Mitochondrial Eve was never mankind's solitary helpmeet. She lived in community with other women, but imagine as the clock starts to click forward that some of these women are barren or lose their children to any one of the manifold dangers of the time or that they produce male children only, then the seeming improbability of the Mitochondrial Eve hypothesis begins to recede. Even if a woman of 140,000 years ago produces a daughter who produces a daughter who produces a daughter, down through countless generations, if just one of those great-great-great-great-great-granddaughters is childless, loses her children young or produces only boys, then the original mother's mitochondrial DNA disappears from the picture at that point. The obvious counter-thrust to this model is: what if that original mother produces three surviving daughters who each produce three surviving daughters, one of whom ups the ante by giving birth to four surviving daughters? In that scenario, wouldn't the disappearance of the original mother's mitochondrial DNA seem less

115

like misfortune and more like carelessness? It's a fair enough point, but it fails to take into account the vast tract of time and the compression of generations between 140,000 years ago and the present, and it also fails to take into account the sad recognition that females are not privileged and may at times be handicapped in the survival lottery. Factor into that model a mere hundred years when female newborns, or even only female twins, were routinely slaughtered or exposed and the model shifts considerably.

So is there no trace left of those women who shared the same sun as Mitochondrial Eve? Very simply, yes. If those women had sons, or sons and daughters, who in turn produced sons and daughters, then their nuclear DNA will have passed down the generations and may still be active, albeit much transformed today, while their mitochondrial DNA is extinct. Mitochondrial Eve, of course, lived in a community of men and women who reproduced in the normal way and with the normal mixed results. Few of these pairings can claim to have established an unbroken line of descent, one of those impressive processions of 'begats' one finds in the Bible, that leads to the present day. But some will have, and somewhere in that descent, much later remember than the 'mt-MRCA', is *the* Most Recent Common Ancestor, the individual from whom everyone alive at the present claims some form of genetic descent. As suggested above, the best current guess is that this 'concestor', as Richard Dawkins describes it, must have lived somewhere in historical times, perhaps as little as a thousand years BC.

There is a seeming paradox lurking here, but it is only a seeming paradox. The Most Recent Common Ancestor lived in a mixed population of humans, some of whom passed on their genome to some of the present human population, though only the MRCA passed on DNA to all of it. It follows that once you have hypothesised an MRCA, its — and it must be it, since neither inevitably he nor she — its parents are also common ancestors. The further back one follows the lineage the more common ancestors turn up until one reaches a point where humanity can be precisely divided into two groups: those who have left no present-day descendants and those who are common ancestors of everyone alive today. This is the so-called 'identical ancestors point'.

These are mind-boggling ideas. The methodology used to arrive at them is heavily questioned as are the (pre)historical implications of the model, but there is an almost mythological purity to the theory and in a search for Eden that necessarily moved along long chronological axes as well as along dusty roads, it exerted a powerful impact.

↪

Cann, Stoneking and Wilson hadn't yet published 'Mitochondrial DNA and human evolution' when I squatted amid the scrub of Oldupai Gorge, now a little more nervous of real and venomous rather than simply iconic snakes, and talked to Adam and Lucy Harding, fellow Eden questers, passionate believers in the theory of African genesis, and kindly faces. It was a chance meeting, but became a strong friendship and I missed them both very much when a few years later, both died within months, of cancers that each had kindly kept concealed from the other.

They took great delight in pointing out and were equally delighted to have pointed out to them, the singular appropriateness of their names. Adam and Eve might have been a little too obvious, but since the earliest fossil find of a pre-modern human who walked upright had been nicknamed 'Lucy', she thought it fit just perfectly, and her sun-browned features crinkled enthusiastically no matter how many times the joke was made.

Adam and Lucy had visited Oldupai many times and were informed and patient guides to the area. They showed me where the Leakeys had begun their patient search, and how the various beds of the dig had been uncovered. We sat and watched a group of herders drift by, watching us in turn with that same neutral expression. The older men carried bows and unfeasibly long arrows, apparently intended to hang from the body of a shot animal, weigh it down and impede its progress until it could be caught.

The Hardings were not scientists; were not, in

fact, conventionally well educated in an academic way. Both were merely – if merely is the word – insatiably curious. They had not yet been to Ethiopia and were fascinated to hear about Rimbaud and the forbidden city. They asked me questions about him as if I knew the poet personally and as if I had personally opened up the interior to white travellers. I suspect they rather enjoyed 'adopting' surrogate sons and daughters on their childless travels. An old army hand, who claimed fluency in an unlikely array of languages (though it always seemed to be Lucy who managed to make herself understood when push came to shove), Adam was an enthusiastic collector of arcane theories, which he seemed neither to believe nor to discount, cheerfully ending each exposition with a philosophical shrug and 'That's what they say, anyway'. He was the first person I heard suggest that Moses and Akhenaten, the founding fathers of monotheism, were one and the same person. He had soaked up all sorts of ideas about UFOs and the role of alien visitors in creating some of the architectural wonders of the ancient world. When we met, they had just travelled south from visiting the pyramids, dismayed at how commercialised the whole Giza experience had become. Adam had been reading new theories about the relationship of the structures to the stars in Orion's belt and had to see for himself.

One thing he did passionately believe was the Garden of Eden had lain somewhere in the Nile basin and that one day it would be rediscovered. As we followed the curve of the ravine, Adam conjured up a place no longer arid and barren, but sufficiently watered and provisioned to sustain a tiny population who probably knew nothing of other peoples, nothing of any other part of the world, whose isolation was probably compounded of more contentment than fear. These were not people who needed to farm or to range further afield than was necessary to bring down some small animal with good meat. This was a community that knew there was danger outside the circle of light and beyond the horizons of immediate need. This was Eden, an experience repeated again and again in our early history and with the same chordal inevitability to its ending. We kicked the dust at our feet, and a curious mournfulness fell over me, as it does whenever I am reminded.

Later, I glimpsed them standing unembarrassed in their underwear under the canopy of their jeep, splashing the dust off each other's shoulders, chatting happily in the setting sun. They exhibited a kind of grace that only comes with absolute unselfconsciousness. Not the first couple, but the only couple in their particular world, locked into a sweet present tense.

∽

The Hardings did not pass on any of their DNA. When the subject of family came up, Adam stoutly declared that it was his fault they hadn't been able to raise one of their own. He hadn't produced enough sperm. 'That's what they said, anyway'. His primal namesake seems in some danger of disappearing from this story, and according to some accounts in danger of disappearing altogether. In a book published a few years after *The Seven Daughters of Eve*, Brian Sykes set out the alarming scenario of 'a future without men'. He called it *Adam's Curse.*

There should, to satisfy our sense of natural order, be a consort for Mitochondrial Eve. Demonstrably, there was one, but we can say virtually nothing about him. Her real male equivalent lived some 30,000 years after her. His curse is in his name, because science knows him as Y-Chromosomal Adam and it is the steady withering of the Y-chromosome that leads Sykes to believe that in a little over 100,000 years (and how cheering to meet a scientist still prepared to give us *any* chance of surviving so long) human reproduction will be an all-female process, requiring eggs to be fertilised with the X-chromosome of another woman. Admirers of feminist science fiction seem thrilled that one of their favourite – indeed, favoured – scenarios seems to be playing out in the real world. But men aren't quite done yet, even if they deserve to be. In the first place, the Y-chromosome does seem capable of repairing itself, so perhaps the decline will be halted. Secondly, some other species have undergone a similar withering and continued to reproduced unchecked; in the kangaroo, the Y-chromosome has been whittled away to just one solitary gene, and kangaroos are still more worried about being turned into meat or shoe leather than they are about genetic extinction. Finally, it's altogether possible that the weakening of the Y-chromosome and declining sperm count are the result of a poisonous industrial environment. If so, that is a historical process dating back only a couple of hundred years and thus at least theoretically reversible, if only we have the will to do it.

So what of the individual who carried this curse? To complicate an already complicated model, the word should be 'individuals', because Y-Chromosomal Adam has changed throughout history. As male lineages die out, someone new becomes the Y-MRCA. Also, these Adams have a far more variable chance of passing on their DNA than their female counterpart. One man might mate successfully with several women or he might through injury, illness or early death father none at all, so the dice are somewhat loaded.

They didn't meet. That's the important thing.

Y-Chromosomal Adam, or at least our present one, lived some 70,000 to 90,000 years ago. Like Mitochondrial Eve, he was not the only one of his sex alive at the time, nor, for the same reasons given above, is he so susceptible to the effects of population bottleneck. Many men living at the same time as the Y-MRCA have descendants alive today, but only Y-MRCA has an unbroken line of male descendants living at this time. He is Adam in a different and perhaps purer sense than Mitochondrial Eve is Eve.

⌇

In the stillness at Oldupai, it is easy enough to feel at the beginning of things. There is a primal loneliness about the place, a silence that assumes almost a physical presence. I had experienced it elsewhere on my travels, in Iran and Turkey, in the dry back country of Bahrain, and at home among deserted crofters' cottages and on St Kilda. It is the particular silence that comes off abandoned places, where hope and promise have in some way been stilled and left behind. There is also a measure of threat in that silence. On my final night, as I tried to sleep, there was a sharp, coughing bark somewhere near at hand. A lion? Or maybe a leopard? I had no particular desire to find out. More alarmingly, given the memory of that snake, I heard occasional rasping slithers.

So I read. I had with me my copy of Pliny's *Historia naturalis*, one of those texts which is fated to be stripped in memory of all but one line: *there is always something new coming out of Africa*. It's seldom accurately attributed and some curious process of back-translation has even rendered the Latin inaccurately, as *Ex Africa semper aliquid novi*, when it ought to be *Semper aliquid novi Africam adferre*. Only a classics master might really mind, but the unwarranted change does give the line a slightly different spin. *Africa is always bringing us something new* is perhaps a better version, and you can hear just a tinge of wry irony in that, particularly when you remember that the phrase has been applied to such terrifying human novelties as jazz rhythms and the AIDS virus.

If modern humans were 'something new', the

exact course of their dispersal out of Africa, out of the shrivelling Eden of the Rift Valley and into Nod beyond is still a matter of controversy. Though there are those who still argue in favour of a multi-regional model, in which human species emerge independently in regions remote from one another, and possibly through hybridisation with older hominid remnants, such a theory fatally lacks convincing DNA evidence. In another phrase consistently misquoted from the *Historia naturalis*, it has to be taken *cum grano salis*.

Most research, and it has been confirmed as recently as 1997 by the results of tests on Neanderthal bones, points to a version of the 'Out of Africa' model, known more prosaically as the Recent Single-Origin Hypothesis. According to this version, primitive hominids evolved in Africa some two million years ago and then migrated outward during one of the climatically suitable periods for dispersal provided by inter-glacial optima when lakes, afforestation and plentiful animal life, or low tidal levels in the Red Sea, would have made these epic journeys feasible.

These wanderers through the Levant and into

Asia and southern Europe became the progenitors of Neanderthal and Java man, impressive civilisations in their own way, but doomed to leave no permanent genetic trace, even when there seem to be similarities with some modern ethnic groups. The RSOH model then proposes that anatomically modern humans evolved in Africa somewhere between 200,000 and 100,000 years ago and then some twenty or twenty-five millennia later, and with similar climatic factors working in their favour, began a second great dispersal. There is no sign of interbreeding with remnant populations of older species, and no hard evidence as to what happened when 'modern' humans encountered those primitive pioneers. Even the most fleeting knowledge of later colonial history colours any likely scenario with pessimism.

⌐

On an earlier evening at Oldupai, I had gone to eat with the Hardings and heard that early history rendered with epic grimness. Long before I read about

Y-Chromosomal Adam or the mt-MRCA, I listened to Adam expounding on 'Pre-Planetary Prince Man', 'Post-Bestowal Son Man' and 'Material Son and Daughter', and on the dark and bloody epoch of mankind's emergence, through which we had come admired throughout the universe for our stoicism and heroism. There seemed no end to Adam's intellectual enthusiasms, which he held with a cheerful suspension of disbelief. It transpired that he and Lucy were avid readers of *The Urantia Book*, a strange blend of Christian cosmology, evolutionary science and a psychological discipline not unlike Scientology's Dianetics.

The book's origins are almost as strange as its contents. No author is named. First published in 1955 and almost twice as long as the King James Bible, *The Urantia Book* purports to have been dictated by the celestial beings who administer a cosmic system of evolution and settlement that leads, by distinct stages, to the Era of Light and Life. If the book has human authors, they are two highly regarded Chicago doctors, William S. Sadler and his wife Lena Kellogg

Sadler. Sometime before the First World War, they were asked to attend an anonymous patient who had entered a curious twilit world, somewhere between sleep and coma. Over time, the so-called 'sleeping subject' began to communicate – the exact process isn't clear – a series of precepts and messages that were transcribed by the Sadlers. Around a dozen years later, the two doctors established a study group called the Forum to discuss the contact personality's revelations. Lest he – or she – were to become the object of a cult, the identity of the source was never revealed. In time, though, the 'sleeping subject' let it be known that it would be possible to question the celestial beings and a smaller group, known as the Contact Commission, was convened to refine a line of enquiry.

Later, presumably when the original 'sleeping subject' was no longer alive, it was suggested that some parts of the eventual text simply manifested themselves by other means. This is a generous way of saying that the Sadlers lifted them wholesale from other sources. For Adam Harding, the best proof of the book's veracity was William Sadler's reputation as a vigorous debunker of all things paranormal. But wasn't that the best possible cover story, I wanted to know. Didn't the most famous picture of the 'Loch Ness Monster' gain substantial credence from being known as 'The Surgeon's Photograph', even though it was clearly dated April 1st and taken (on the Serpentine, it turns out) by a well-known practical joker? As ever, Adam shrugged amicably. 'That's what they say, at any rate.'

Urantia is, of course, the Earth. It is one of the inhabited planets of the local universe Nebadon, which in turn is part of the superuniverse Orvonton, from whose capital Uversa the commission responsible for dictating the 'Urantia Papers' hails. By the standards of its time, the proposed cosmology is relatively sophisticated, combining early 20th century astrophysics with something like the medieval concept of 'spheres'. At the centre of the system are the billion perfect worlds of Havona, the Sacred Spheres of Paradise, twenty-one giant worlds organised in three tiers of seven, and at the very hub, the Isle of Paradise, where God resides, omniscient, perfect, infinite and the embodiment of love, communicating with every individual through a 'Thought Adjuster', inner spirit or daimon.

So far, so consistent with any one of a dozen New Age religions. The most fascinating aspect of *The Urantia Book* is its blend of Darwinism, eugenics and celestial intervention, reconciling Biblical creation with the stumbling block of the fossil record. According to the system it proposes, each planet within the habitable range has been seeded with organic life which has been coded to evolve towards intelligence and free will. This is not necessarily an orderly or continuous process. It can be interrupted by error on the part of the celestial ministers or by deliberate rebellion. This is the case on Urantia, where it is taught the emergence of 'will dignity' has been severely hampered by the prideful revolt of Caligastia who arrived as planetary prince 500,000 years ago but gave his loyalty to the anarchic libertarianism of Lucifer, the ruler of Satania. The 'Lucifer Rebellion' led Satania to be quarantined from the rest of the universe, while the chaos of Caligastia's uprising on

Urantia set humanity back countless generations in its movement towards light and life. It seems that Jesus, in his role as son of the Creator, allowed all this to take place, watching and waiting for millennia as mankind steadily worked its way back to the true path.

When Caligastia came to Earth/Urantia, he founded his princedom between the rivers Tigris and Euphrates, in Mesopotamia. It's tempting to think that this is where *The Urantia Book* puts the seat of Eden, but the story is more complicated than that. A key stage in the evolution of fully conscious humans is the arrival of a 'Material Son and Daughter', incarnated representatives of the celestial power whose descent will effectuate the great jump forward. These are Adam and Eve. They are not, however, the first named man and woman. That role goes to Andon and Fonta, a brother and sister who decide to live apart from their contemporaries and whose incestuous offspring evolve into modern humans. They live as hunter-gatherers, with only minimal religious awareness, and their era is characterised by violence

133

and want. The 'Pre-Planetary Prince' era on Urantia is said to have been bloodier than most, and much longer, which may have predisposed Urantia's human population to rebellion.

Caligastia was still in conflict with the Creator's spirit when Adam and Eve came to Urantia, some 40,000 years ago. Their first act is to build – note that it is not God but they who do it – a Garden of Eden, which *The Urantia Book* places on a now-submerged peninsula jutting out into the Mediterranean Sea from the Holy Land, thus conflating Eden with Atlantis. Their mission on Urantia is to breed a species of advanced humans who will in the fullness of time interbreed with the evolved population and stimulate a dramatic 'biological uplift'.

Tragically, though, they have been sent to a world signally unprepared to make a step forward and denied sustaining contact with the rest of the universe because of Caligastia's rebellion. Eve despairs of their task and to bring forward their mission mates directly with one of the primitives. When Adam learns of her crime, he decides to share her fate and does the same. Their punishment is mortality. Adam and Eve are denied the fruits of the Tree of Life. When surrounding tribes learn what has happened, they attack Eden and destroy the garden. Adam, Eve and their children are driven out and obliged to build a second Eden elsewhere, now cursed with the foreknowledge of death as well as sexual shame.

It's a powerful variant on the old myth, and a very American one. The epical strain, the grand imperial conflict, the obsessions with miscegenation and sexual hygiene, the uneasy but shameless mix of scientific humanism and mysticism – all give it away as a this-worldly artefact, and a New Worldly one at that. The Hardings expressed surprise when I told them I had never visited America, where another of the great Christian revisionist movements, one far more successful than the Urantians, puts the site of Paradise. Adam and Lucy were, unsurprisingly, also fascinated by *The Book of Mormon*, though as Adam gallantly put it, he had no interest in polygamy, being married already to the best girl in the world. We talked a little about Columbus and where he believed he had made that fateful landfall. Some have argued that he called the indigenous population 'Indians' not because he really believed he had reached the fabled East, but because on American shores he found a people living *in Dios*, in God. A charming conceit, but one that somehow doesn't quite sit with Columbus's psychological profile.

There have always been reasons not to visit America – political, financial, a dislike of flying, the mixture of fear and tedium that followed the World Trade Center attacks and turned 'homeland security' into a new brand of isolationism. At bottom, though, I am an inhabitant of the Old World, uninterested in frontiers, always convinced that the real answer to any question lies not two steps ahead but behind us and overlooked. I had come close to some version of Eden, or as I increasingly thought of it, to the Edenic experience, several times in my travels, here in Africa very intimately and with greater backing from science, but never closer and never more powerfully than that first time in the south-east of Turkey. So I went back ...

6

The beast clings to its pillar, head down, tail powerfully lashed, its expression forbidding. Precisely what sort of creature it is remains unclear. The skin and head suggest something reptilian, but it has the heavy haunches of a leopard. Perhaps it is a mythological hybrid. Even carved out of limestone and blurred by centuries of burial and lime deposit, it has a dismaying dynamism, a quality that goes deep into the psyche and finds an echo in all of us, some atavistic recall of a moment when our innocence was lost.

～

First discovered in 1963, the site is about eight

miles north east of Urfa in south eastern Turkey. The name Gobekli Tepe means 'hill with a navel', which is immediately redolent since in the Middle Ages gallons of ink were spilt over the question of whether Adam and Eve, created directly by God rather than born of woman, had the distinctive remnant of an umbilical cord. Generations of artists, perhaps devoted to anatomical accuracy rather than carefully finessed theology, decided that they had.

Gobekli Tepe sits on top of a limestone ridge on a spur of the Taurus mountains. The man-made mound is about 50 feet high and 300 yards round, and contains one of the oldest stone temples yet uncovered, dating to some 10,000 years BC. That figure, confirmed by radiocarbon dating, means that the site is of staggering antiquity. Most non-specialists have only the haziest notion of pre-historic chronology. Suffice it to say that probably the best known archaeological monument in the British Isles, Stonehenge, was constructed a mere 3,000 years BC. The dating of Gobekli Tepe is significant not just for its great age, but also because it means that the complex construction was made by hunter-gatherers, violating a long-held principle that elaborate stone building only took place after the transition to agriculture and the beginning of a more static, though still inevitably shifting, way of human life. Genetic evidence suggests that Gobekli Tepe lay within the region where the first domesticated cereals were first cultivated and where the first domesticated pigs were reared – the former a rough wheat known as *einkorn*, the latter narrowed down to Cayonu, not much more than an hour away – though as yet no trace of farmed animals or domesticated foodstuffs has been found at the site. Even so, its apparent contradiction of the received chronology may provide a clue to its precise point and purpose. Perhaps it was here that hunting-gathering began to give way to organised planting, by way of some transitional process whereby the collection of wild grains and berries was socially organised. That, at least, is the opinion of Dr Klaus Schmidt of the University of Heidelberg, who since 1995 has been directing the excavation. In one regard it is a curious dig, because it reverses an opposite, and equally deliberate, process. Gobekli Tepe was not submerged by blown sand or volcanic ash, generations of silts and other debris. It was filled in, sometime around a millennium after its first construction.

There are many mysteries surrounding Gobekli Tepe, but there are one or two certainties. German archaeologists from Karlsruhe who have investigated the site are clear that the buildings were not houses. There is no evidence of human habitation, which suggests that the construction was of ritual significance. The buildings are round and made of dry stone with floors made of burnt lime or terrazzo. Around the outer walls are shallow benches, which may have been intended for sitting, or for leaving sacrifices. The walls are punctuated by ten foot high carved pillars in the shape of the Greek *tau* or our **T** and it is on these that Gobekli Tepe's remarkable gallery of animals can be found.

Here are to be found, in carved relief, lions, boars and foxes, ducks and herons, snakes and ants, animals that may well have had some totemic significance to those who built the place. There are sculptures in addition, again of animals. Some of the reliefs have been deliberately chipped away. There is no definite explanation for the defacement. Perhaps some of the animals depicted were implicated in some perceived act of betrayal against the temple-builders. Perhaps the carvings had been damaged and were intended to be replaced. Like perhaps the majority of the most significant locations in the archaeological record, Gobekli Tepe asks more questions than it answers.

⌐

I returned to Turkey older (obviously), no wiser than I should have been, and both physically and mentally exhausted. But I also returned with a conviction that what had happened in a tiny garden in an anonymous hamlet near Urfa eighteen years before may have been something more than a purely personal epiphany, perhaps a quiet intimation of something more profound.

I spent a quiet evening in Urfa with two young American archaeology students, Maryanne Selig and Karl Bosch, whose efforts *not* to behave like a couple made them seem ever more besotted. Both were Christians and bible scholars, though without the evangelical zeal of the born-again. They took their science seriously, cautious about the evidence, and resonantly sceptical as to conclusions. But, even before such speculations were made widely public, both were convinced that the region around Gobekli Tepe had some connection to the Eden story and to other aspects of the Genesis narrative.

On our first day there, they gave me a lift in an ancient jeep, not to the excavation itself, but southeast to Harran. The name had rung a faint bell when Karl mentioned it the night before. Also known as Carrhae, and part of Sanliurfa province, which closely abuts the Syrian border, Haran is mentioned in Genesis. By now, I was relatively cautious about the seeming coincidence of place-names, which often sounds a deceptive harmonic in archaeological research, but the name is derived from the Akkadian *haranu*, which means 'pathway' or 'journey' and there is a long-standing tradition that Adam and Eve passed through the place after the expulsion from Eden. It is mentioned twice in Genesis itself, first in chapter xi where Haran is the father of Lot but also the place, identified as being in Canaan, where Terah, Abram, Lot and their wives and children live after leaving Ur of the Chaldees. Some legends also confusingly identify Harran with Ur. It is mentioned again in chapter xxvii, when Rebekah tells Jacob to flee to Haran to escape the murderous wrath of his brother Esau.

The town's standing as a cultural hub was reinforced in the 8th century when the first Islamic university was established there, a recognised centre for mathematics and astronomy. Though nominally Christian, the town and its environs seem to have retained a loyalty to the old pagan religion and a distinctive culture known as Sabianism sprang up there, only overturned around 1033 when famine in the countryside led to Harran being sacked by starving farmers in league with Muslim militia. Harran was also a key location during the Crusades, when the town was besieged by Baldwin II of Edessa, with

Tancred of Galilee and Bohemond of Antioch, three of the most powerful of the crusading princes. In an apparent bid to lure the investing force away, the Seljuk Turks marshalled a large army a day and half's march away at Ra's al-'ain, where on 7 May 1104 the Crusaders suffered one of their first major defeats.

The modern town is precisely that. The distinctive adobe 'beehive' houses are nowadays preserved as picturesque heritage remnants rather than dwelling places, though I read later that some of the houses would still have been inhabited when I first visited the region in 1977. Like much of the Fertile Crescent, the area has gone through succeeding periods of fertility and drought, the latest turnaround in its agricultural fortunes brought about by human intervention. After the rivers Deysan and Cullab dried up, withered with overuse, a vast irrigation project for southern Anatolia restored its farming infrastructure, while more locally drilling projects accessed some of the deeper aquifers. As we drove in, we again passed carts crammed with workmen heading out to the fields. Cotton is an important crop, and rice is grown here as well, but on a smaller scale the region feeds itself generously.

The same project, known as the Guneydogu Anadolu Projesi, has also developed hydro-electric power schemes on the Tigris and Euphrates, which rise in the region. The presence of these rivers, at almost any point from source to mouth, is of iconic significance in the search for Eden, but there always remains the question of how to identify the other two rivers mentioned in Genesis. In this context, the Deysan and Cullab will not work, but some researchers, including Michael Sanders, who has specialised in the solution of biblical mysteries, are clear that the mysterious Gihon and Pishon are readily identified as the northern branch of the Euphrates and the Murat river, also known as the Arsanias, which is a major headstream of the Euphrates, rising near Mt Ararat at Lake Van.

By now, it is fairly clear that any attempt to make the modern map square with Genesis calls for a subtle mixture of research and wishful thinking, as well as a willingness to overlook or rationalise any apparent inconsistency in the original narrative. The Sanders argument tends to ignore the Bible's insistence that the four rivers flow together into Eden, though some have argued that potential ambiguities of perspective – whether Eden is a larger region that contains the garden, whether the viewpoint is Adam's and Eve's or more omniscient, whether there is a potential confusion about the water's direction, where it flows *from,* where it flows *to,* all of these perfectly possible in an ancient text that has undergone successive transcription and translation – have complicated the picture unnecessarily. Set such concerns aside even for a moment and the region, with its fringe of mountains, does in many respects accord with the traditional picture.

⌐

The excavation of Gobekli Tepe had only begun in earnest on that return trip to Turkey, but Selig, Bosch and I were able to view what had the makings of a strikingly dramatic site. It was clear that something

important was concealed there and that the concealment was deliberate. As the decade slowly wound
towards the millennium, an obvious epoch in any
field related to Christian history and pre-history,
the finds became ever more dramatic and a certain
consensus began to emerge as to what Gobekli Tepe
might mean.

One of the most dramatic carvings shows what
appear to be water-birds being caught in a net. This,
plus the many images of game animals, points to a
conclusion: that the site was created in celebration
of a hunting-gathering lifestyle. The location shows
signs of sustained and complex building activity,
which must have involved many hundreds, possibly
thousands of people. Traces of tools have been found
there, confirming those numbers. Sensoring has
shown that there are more than 200 standing stones
in the vicinity, and an unfinished pillar, taller than
any at the site itself, has been found at a quarry half
a mile away.

A certain model begins to emerge from these
findings. If a great many people were involved in

building and maintaining the original temple, even just in visiting it occasionally, then clearly these people would need to have been fed. For a hunting-gathering community, this would have had a steady and probably irreversible impact on the natural environment. Hunting-gathering is a way of life that depends absolutely on the modern concept of sustainability. Put too much pressure on the local ecology, whether by felling trees, stripping fruits and nuts, or killing animals, and that ecology will eventually collapse. This may well be what happened at Gobekli Tepe. If a major cult were associated with the place and one that involved large numbers of people, the impact on the surrounding countryside would have been considerable. What Klaus Schmidt has argued is that if the usual means of acquiring food were exhausted by a population reluctant to abandon a location that clearly had a profound social, cultural, spiritual and possibly aesthetic significance, then this may have triggered some attempt to harness food plants or animals. Other local evidence, such as the first use of *einkorn* wheat and the domestication of wild pigs, suggests that Gobekli Tepe witnessed the emergence of planned agriculture.

The principle of simultaneous evolution applies here as it does to so many aspects of the human story. It is always treacherously dangerous to apply the word 'first' in cultural history. An awkward and inconsistent regress almost always delivers a prior example or related case. There may well be other Gobekli Tepes dotted across the region, each of them in some way marking the high point and subsequent decline of a paradisal way of life which demanded no organised labour or food 'industry'.

⤶

It is always difficult to separate one's sense of a place from one's state of mind when it is first visited. To that extent, I am hardly surprised that I remember Gobekli Tepe with a more than faint melancholy, since I was unmistakably depressed on that visit. I have only returned once since, to a far more developed excavation, and having seen a substantial literature emerge about its potential significance. Leaving aside its speculative relation to the Eden story, Gobekli Tepe is arguably the most important archaeological site in recent history, while its aesthetic beauty places it, for some at least, on a par with the cave paintings at Lascaux, also dominated by the getting of food. Perhaps by association of ideas, perhaps in response to something deeper, I felt immediately sombre on returning to the site. The sun blazed down, beating off the limestone dust with a strength that was almost audible. The senior archaeologists responsible for briefing visiting journalists were palpably excited by their work, and full of confidence that Gobekli Tepe would continue to yield up, perhaps delivering answers, perhaps merely opening up new mysteries.

And yet I felt an immediate lowering of the spirits, an almost elegiac sense of loss that seemed sharply at odds with the surroundings. Or it may have been an unconscious reaction to the temple's eventual fate, for the way of life celebrated there was fated to end. Somewhere between 1,000 and 2,000 years after the structures were first built, someone took the trouble to drag tons of limey dirt to that small hill and to bury a structure that had taken years of phenomenal effort to build. This doesn't look like an act of iconoclasm, the furious vandalism of apostates or non-believers. It has an air of weary resignation about it, this gesture, regret rather than anger, perhaps a tinge of mourning, maybe shame as well.

One can imagine those for whom the temple was once the focus of their lives, a simple celebration of ease and plenty, one day recognising that it had fallen into disuse, that the old cult no longer squared with immediate realities. Here was a people that now had to live by the sweat of their brows, battling against blights and depleted soils, fearing drought, not yet sufficiently aware of the chemistry of humus to be able to correct its deficiencies. Where before they had lived in a spontaneous symbiosis with other animal species, hunting and perhaps occasionally hunted in return – for surely that crouching figure on the pillar looks powerful enough to take an incautious man? – but in a complex harmony with nature, now they found themselves forced into an aggressive territoriality, scaring away the birds that plucked up ungerminated seed and the beasts that trampled the rising crops. Where before they had shared wild game with other predators, now they had to protect domesticated animals from the same creatures. A basic contract with the earth was violated. So with lowered brows and averted eyes, they put from sight the living symbol of a squandered paradise.

∽

I was perversely pleased, or perhaps relieved, to learn that Bosch shared my sense of sorrow on visiting the place. In later letters he described Gobekli Tepe as beautiful but ineffably sad, the sadness coming not so much from those painstakingly constructed buildings and sculptures, whose discovery had at a stroke required archaeology to recalibrate its timelines, but by the fact of their subsequent concealment. We agreed that if there were an objective correlative to mankind's fall into shame, it was even deeper than the sexual unease which is the founding principle of psychoanalysis and which seems to come down the headstreams and tributaries of the Judaeo-Christian tradition, all the way from Genesis to Freud, symbolised by serpents, fig-leaves, flaming swords turning this way and that.

Satan takes many forms, cormorant, toad, snake, so it is not impossible that that ambiguous carving, clasped upside down on its pillar, does not already represent some force at work in nature that, unless resisted, will breach the accord of Eden.

∾

Perhaps the temple has an elegiac purpose, celebrating and mourning the end of simple plenty.

7

The house appears to float between sky and shore, perched halfway up the hillside. Its neighbours have crumbled, or have been despoiled to repair walls and bottom out washed-away roads. They are hard to find now, often no more than random sprawls of anomalously even stone, but once nearly 1,000 souls lived here and scraped a living from the acid soil. At sunset, the shadows of old runrigs emerge briefly, legacy of a time when good ground and poor was distributed evenly among the community, guarantee that no one family enjoyed a fertile patch while another struggled to coax barley or potatoes out of a rushy, waterlogged dip.

There are stories of massacres here, ancient rivalries and hatreds, and the farm stands close to a ridge-line of market stones that once demarcated two kingdoms, owing allegiance to Alcluith (Dumbarton Rock) in the 'British' east and to Dunadd in the 'Scottish' west. Past slaughters are still commemorated, but there is little talk here of Clearance and the elaborate victim-mythology that comes with it. Most of the 1,000 or so who left, did so willingly and with glad hearts, disappearing into the factories and shipyards of Glasgow, or on emigrant boats to America, Canada and Australia. Perhaps some 'Scottish passengers' set sail dreaming of Eden in Tasmania. There is a small historical irony in their departure, for the discovery that liberal applications of lime sweetened the soil meant that this land could have been farmed if not profitably then at least sustainingly and, in the contemporary parlance, sustainably.

The nearest archaeological relic is a lime-kiln, a circular structure collapsed in on itself, drowned in sand like the structures at Gobekli Tepe and colonised by rabbits. Further afield, there are standing stones, most now recumbent thanks to impatient 'improvers' who wanted their ploughlines straight. Their sockets can be found nearby and there are places where there are sockets with no neighbouring stone, presumably because those same improvers needed a new lintel for a barn or slabs for a cowshed floor and took them from near at hand. In the woods, there are carved markings on the rocks, cup and ring devices whose meaning is still conjecture. On the sharp sides of the glen, again only visible in certain lights and seasons, are recessed platforms, re-used by succeeding generations of herders and charcoal burners, and perhaps by the young men of the clan who once carried dead chiefs along the coffin road past the farm and over a distant shoulder to where they lie together. On hard nights, when the rain drives or when sudden mists descend, these platforms must have offered welcome relief.

Four streams pass through and around the place and meet up below us to flow into the sea. When the rains fall hard, a reddish stain fans out at their common mouth, colouring the water with old blood. Split rocks sometimes reveal semi-precious crystals, but quartzes, white, rosy and grey, are the only abundant treasure. Still, if you have the patience to take a shallow pan down into the gravel and spend a musing half hour swirling it gently round and round, it's not unusual to find gold, not the rich seams of Havilah but tiny flakes as insubstantial as dander.

There is some food to be had from the land. Mushrooms in the woods in autumn, if you have the patience to tease away the moss to look for chanterelles underneath, brambles in the ditches, blueberries on the hill, occasional bounties of hazelnut when we happen across a tree that hasn't yet been stripped by the red squirrels who run around with ears like antennae, always fleeing the encroaching greyness. Wild garlic and sorrel are there for flavouring and we pore over old books that recommend such-and-such a plant for dyeing wool and another for curing ague and quinsy, knowledge that we rarely apply and still more rarely with any success.

The snakes are a cliché, of course, but they are here too, an occasional adder sunning on a flat stone, or the harmless shock of turning up a snake-like slow worm under a dry log or in the compost heap. The real serpents are the rabbits who play delightedly outside our windows and then treacherously eat their way through a whole planting. There is, of course, revenge or symbiosis or our version of the circle of life. They eat a planting. We eat them. The same goes for the wood pigeons who come down and strip the cabbages. And there are fish and shellfish in the sea, best eaten cautiously and when the water is cold and free from poisonous blooms.

Friends come and look around and describe it as idyllic. So it is, but idylls in a fallen world demand the hardest work. We drag up seaweed from the shore and bring down bracken from the hill. They're laid in long lazy-beds – the word comes from *laissez* and carries no imputation of idleness – where they are sandwiched with barrow-loads of sand borrowed from the rabbits. These rot down over the winter and provide fertile mounds for our potatoes, which come up clean and with the faintest tang of iodine.

This is the ancestral curse, a genetic drive to make sour ground give forth. It is back-breaking work, and without end. Fallow soil is immediately recolonized by the brackens, reeds, rank weeds and gorse that surround us in a speckled tangle, like wild animals waiting for a weary traveller to fall asleep and the firelight to dim. Farming here calls for patience and vigilance in equal measure.

It is also important that I write here. If the definition of a crofter is someone who does something else as well as farming, then making text is my equivalent of fishing, or of hunting game. Rebuilding this place has been very much like creating a narrative, its syntax and lexicon inherited but wrested into new shapes. I would, frankly, rather write about the soil than bury my hands in it, chop weeds and hack down straggling growth; but when I catch that chocolatey smell on fingers, see a row cleared of docks and thistles, spot the first curl of a bean-shoot coming through the ground, I would rather do anything in the world rather than write.

During my short time as an academic, it was a

basic article of literary criticism that 'the text' was a distinct thing, entire, iconic and 'autotelic' (I think was the term), and that it was naïve to expect any kind of equivalence to external reality, let alone psychology and morality. Such a viewpoint requires a more sophisticated philosophical nature than I can claim. Though I dimly sense that the table in front of me is not a solid object at all, but a shimmer of nuclei, quarks, bosons and mysterious forces, I am still able to put my elbows on it and gaze out the window. I am not so sure about this old chair, which complains and sways, as if those same adhesive forces were ready to give up at any moment. What I see outside may also be a screen of illusions, but unlike Dr Johnson I don't need to kick any rocks; the mud I routinely drag in on my feet is refutation enough.

I understand and appreciate the complexities inherent in the narratology of Eden. It is a tale told in accessible form that renders down countless generations of mediated experience into a form that somehow communicates to peoples of vastly different experience. Of all the world's peoples, only perhaps the Inuit (and Hugh Brody's argument confirms and denies this by turns) might find the symbolism of Eden alien to their experience. Even a seventh-generation city dweller (a straight descendant of Cain) still defines his or her experience against some deep memory of the garden, which is why we cultivate hostas and geraniums in soilless compost on our balconies, stroll in public parks, and take holidays where the vegetation is flagrantly lush.

Eden is a text, something written and thus inherently untrustworthy. It is also a plain record, abraded and botched by time, of our earthly existence at its turning point.

~

As I write, the spring birds are already in conference. Grey wagtails strut importantly around the yard in their morning dress and yellow waistcoats. Wrens yell from niches in the stone walls. The resident barn owl, who looks down irritably from the beams of an old cowshed, is resigned to making her hunting flights in a shortening night. A pair of cuckoos dash to and fro, pulling us away from work when they call unexpectedly close, then calling again from the far side of the old runrigs before we have reached for the binoculars. We see them from time to time, swinging their long tails on a fencepost or making the low, fast flights that make them hard to distinguish from the sparrow-hawks who panic the song birds. They prey on finches and tits, making stealthy passes down the line of the burn before coming in blind and unbelievably fast over the lower wall to take a straggler. Only the long-tailed tits, who feed in packs of a dozen or more, making a call that sounds like bunches of tiny keys being shaken, seem to have devised a way of avoiding them. The most common local raptors are buzzards, who lament ceaselessly overhead and wait for roadkill or perhaps a rabbit that wasn't picked up after a lamping. There are golden eagles further up the glen, who make a daily sortie down its flanks, irritating the buzzards and crows but magnificently indifferent to their presence. We have had visits from osprey and once, breath-takingly, from a prospecting sea eagle down from the Outer Hebrides and still wearing its orange release tag. Once, a tiny merlin peered down from a tree.

Halfway to the shore is a tree the woodpeckers seem to favour, drumming there on still days, attended by tiny treecreepers who inch jerkily down the trunks looking for the smallest insects. Pass through the gate to the beach and the common gulls who nest there take off in alarm, leaving their eggs in barely insulated hollows in the gravel. The oystercatchers are braver, hopping off sideways until one takes flight and the rest follow. The sandpipers who arrive back from Africa and the Levant about now let us come within feet of where they stand before they explode into action and disappear behind the next neck of gravel on whirring wings. The ringed plovers have a different strategy. They simply keep a distance, visible only when they move, seeming to vanish in an instant when they keep still against the pebbly background.

It was here, as a boy, that I saw a hoopoe, not the loud and officious bird of Attar's great poem, but a bedraggled traveller who'd clearly lost his way in the gales. He bounced along the tideline where snow bunting sometimes feed in winter, with a lethargic alarm. He was gone the next day, perhaps taken by a hawk, perhaps re-oriented and bound for his proper destination.

~

We're all in some way battered migrants, brought home again by some emotional magnetism and dead reckoning. It took me thirty years and a certain amount of storm and wrack to return to this place. A further banishment is entirely possible. Landlords are more capricious than deities and wield very similar powers. Our list of prohibitions, particularly during shooting season, makes Eden look positively *laissez-faire.* And yet the very precariousness of our contract with the place, the sheer, unremitting slog of extracting a living from this land are precisely what binds us to it. *In the sweat of thy face shalt thou eat bread, till thou return unto the ground ...*

We are three now and while the boy is perfectly capable of raising Cain, we prefer to think of him as our Seth, a child of age and, with luck and justice, the sustainer of a line. This place is, say visiting friends, a boy's paradise, little knowing how deeply that resonates.

⤻

After much travel and long search, do I honestly believe that I have rediscovered Eden? I react to the question almost as abrasively as those biblical students who react to each new archaeological finding with the same furious response 'Of course they haven't uncovered the site of Eden, *Because. It. Was. Swept. Away. In. The. Flood!!*' but in doing so entirely miss a rich irony: that a secular scientist should even be talking about the Garden of Eden at all, let alone discussing its possible location.

It's a question with two parts, and with respective answers yes and no. If, as seems probable, Eden represents the purest retelling of an actual experience

165

common to almost every early human population, then Edens existed across Africa, Southern Asia and the Fertile Crescent, flourishing in areas that are now no more than squabbled-over sand. It may be that in ancient times there was one legendary garden that seemed to outstrip all others in fertility and abundance, or it may be that one garden was simply lucky enough to be memorialised in a surviving text, or it may be that the Genesis scribe, learned in other creation myths now lost to us or handed down in ever-diminishing fragments, condensed a common experience into a story of archetypal simplicity. But this is to muddle a conclusion. There is Genesis as text, and as text it is sublime; and there is Genesis as a subtly encoded historical record. The problem with contemporary analytics is that narratology is quietly permitted to eclipse the real experience that lies behind the text and gives it life.

Eden was real, and the most convincing proof is neither textual nor archaeological, but deeply inscribed on the heart. We sense its reality in an unwilled remembering of past time. It is a memory that many of us may have lost forever, like a vestigial organ rendered obsolete by evolution. Others, sensing that it is fading, try desperately to reproduce it: build communes, go back to the land, turn Green or ecological or environmentalist. The very existence of these movements is itself a symptom of the deep fracture in our relationship with the earth. Instead of a natural and easeful dance, we lunge at Gaia and bruise her with an awkward embrace.

I was, predictably, one of the first to make the trek down to Cornwall to visit the much-vaunted Eden Project. Here, surely, was an initiative that might allow us to answer yes to the second aspect of that question about 'rediscovering' paradise, in the sense of recreating its conditions. I stayed long enough to justify the entrance price and came away sadly. The car radio was playing 'Big Yellow Taxi', not the Joni Mitchell original significantly, but an anodyne pop queen of the moment. The lyric, though, matched my mood precisely: *'They paved Paradise / And put up a parking lot'*; only here they had turned Eden into a theme park, with a parking lot alongside. They do fine work there, and it may be that with climate change and runaway habitat destruction some plant species may rely on this and similar projects for their continued existence but there is something emotionally unsatisfying about an oversize hothouse.

If only it could break free of its earthbound existence. The Eden Project immediately made me think of Douglas Trumbull's ecological science fiction fantasy *Silent Running*, one of the cult films of my teens. Made in 1971, it is set in 2001, a fairly obvious reference, since Trumbull created many of the special effects for Stanley Kubrick's *2001: A Space Odyssey*; unused effects were pressed into service for his own film. Bruce Dern plays Freeman Lowell, a caftaned space-botanist responsible for maintenance of a huge space-ark intended to repopulate an Earth scorched and emptied by nuclear war. It seems an idyllic life, a hippie dream. He lives and works in grouchy disagreement with his more cynical crewmates on the *Valley Forge*, but for the tiny robots over whom he has, apparently, more secure dominion than the astronauts in *2001* had over their malevolent onboard computer. There is, inevitably, a complication. Lowell is told that his project has been decommissioned and is ordered to destroy with nuclear charges the huge geodesic domes that hold the world's last forests. Lowell jettisons some of the domes as a ruse and kills his crew members, human company replaced by three obedient drones, Huey, Dewey and Louie. They save his life when he reprogrammes them to perform surgery and the ship leaves the freighter fleet on course for Saturn (which was the original location for the events of *2001* before technical problems enforced a change to Jupiter). As they move out through the solar system, Lowell's beloved forest starts to wither and die. It seems improbable that a trained botanist would fail to recognise the symptoms of sunlight deprivation on photosynthesising plants.

The recognition comes too late to save Lowell himself. The *Valley Forge* has been tracked down by a sister ship, which is close to docking. Lowell rigs up huge banks of ultraviolet lights to save his trees and plants and leaving the last surviving drone – Louie and Huey have been lost or destroyed – to tend the forest blows up the *Valley Forge* and himself. The final scene shows the solitary Dewey working with a child's watering can as Lowell's ecological 'message in a bottle' drifts out into the darkness.

For all its sentimentality and forced humour – Lowell also reprogrammes the drones to play stud poker – the film's power comes from deep mythic sources. Lowell is a kind of Adam, of course, but Adam after the banishment, desperately trying to recreate Eden in the Nod of outer space. He is also Cain, a murderer who conceals the body of a brother-astronaut. And, ultimately, he is Noah, too. The deeper truths of the Eden story lie in the banishment – the knowledge that where good and evil both exist, we can only know good *by* evil – and in the Flood, which brings the world back to its primal purity for a time at least. The Genesis story marks an end rather than a beginning, or at best marks a transition to a harder and more restless way of life. As a narrative it seems to us essentially elegiac and, in the proper sense, elegiac. It is not so much tragic and tragicomic, which is where Milton's fixation on Satan rather than Adam led the story adrift.

Genesis also offers a paradigm for destruction and for the kind of 'extinction event' now more or less universally accepted by palaeontologists. Biblical literalists have it relatively easy. Whereas UFO buffs have to invent complex technological reasons – invisibility shields, fourth-dimension travel – why aliens do not routinely make themselves known to us when they so obviously crowd our skies, those who accept the Genesis story as an accurate description of our origins are quick to dismiss any suggestion that Eden – or as I have argued, one of many Edens – has actually been found by pointing out that it was simply swept away in the Flood, obliterating its walls and silting up its river courses.

There is always a frisson of mutual unease when science and religion seem to inhabit common ground. Christian fundamentalists react with hostility when archaeologists dare to suggest they have found the site of Eden, almost as if Paradise were just another turf war. They react with similar irritability when other scientists warn what will happen when – and it now seems like when, rather than if – the polar icecaps melt, or the earth is struck by an asteroid or comet. It may be that the Flood is simply a dramatic compression of the Neolithic Wet Phase, which drowned large areas of the fertile Middle East, but it's impossible to rule out something more dramatic, and it is certainly another area where the scientific record seems to confirm the essential veracity of another aspect of biblical text. Even so, the more likely explanation is that advanced by David Rohl, which suggests that a flood simply drowned the houses and covered the urban mounds, and that Noah simply packed family and stock aboard a cannily constructed raft and found himself back on dry land somewhere far to the west.

The winter rains beat down with apocalyptic ferocity, gouging away at precious topsoil and turning tracks into muddy torrents. Foolish but resourceful Noah is perhaps a more convincing model than Adam, even Adam clothed with shame and cast out of the garden. That is not to say that we are survivalists, watching the clouds or peering nervously at the television news in fearful anticipation of disaster, eyeing the roads and boundaries for signs of imminent attack. Rather, we spend our days gathering things up and preserving them, keeping them close to hand. Our pervading sense is similar to that of the crew of the sky-ship 'Inconvenience' in Thomas Pynchon's *Against the Day*, which 'has transformed into its own destination, where any wish that can be made is at least addressed, if not always granted. For every wish to come true would mean that in the known Creation, good unsought and uncompensated would have evolved, somehow, to become at least more accessible to us'.

This is the spirit one imbibes in searching for Eden and what it means, a sense of life rooted in possibility that will mostly be denied, potential that will mostly be thwarted, love that will mostly fall short of its true intentions and fall infertile to one side of its proper furrow. It is a life that is governed by the certainty of failure and the equal certainty of renewed hope in a following season. Of all those mythologically cursed with inaccessible and unattainable goals

– Sisyphus, Tantalus – the sons and daughters of Adam and Eve are the most rigorously denied, but also the most stoically self-possessed. We may not fly towards grace, like Pynchon's sky-pilgrims, but we will eventually feel the keel grate on something solid and come to a halt as the water recedes. It is that moment we anticipate, as we stand here watching the wind, listening to the threatening grumble of the clouds and smelling the air for some portent of the oncoming deluge. We scan the sky for rain, but in expectation of the rainbow.